HOW TO SURVIVE A
Toxic Boss

BY DR. HERRON KEYON GASTON

RoseDog Books
PITTSBURGH, PENNSYLVANIA 15238

The contents of this work including, but not limited to, the accuracy of events, people, and places depicted; opinions expressed; permission to use previously published materials included; and any advice given or actions advocated are solely the responsibility of the author, who assumes all liability for said work and indemnifies the publisher against any claims stemming from publication of the work.

RoseDog Books
585 Alpha Drive
Suite 103
Pittsburgh, PA 15238
Visit our website at *www.rosedogbookstore.com*

ISBN: 979-8-89027-097-9
eISBN: 979-8-89027-595-0

TABLE OF CONTENTS

Chapter 1:
WHAT MAKES A WORKPLACE TOXIC?

Business leaders in the United States knew 2021 as the year of the Great Resignation. It started in April, when 2.7% of the workforce quit, the highest single-month quit rate since these statistics started being recorded. This only increased over the year, hitting a new record high of 3% in September. The causes of this trend are complex and varied, but there's no debating the results: employees stayed at companies that took care of and valued their workers, and left companies that didn't. This was a trend that started well before 2020, though the pandemic accelerated it as people re-evaluated their priorities, or saw companies laying off workers or cutting pay at the same time they were bringing in record profits.

Low-paying positions, especially those in industries like food service and retail, were hit the hardest by this trend. This led many to cite compensation as the driving force of the Great Resignation, but while these no doubt played a role, not everyone who quit did so for better pay. Some went to jobs that paid the same—or even took a pay cut—to escape a bad boss, unhealthy work environment, or exploitative culture. The truth is that the low pay of these positions was a symptom of a deeper ill: that employees in these companies are not respected or valued. It is the toxicity of these environments that's driving workers away in droves.

Toxic workplaces can happen in any industry and can take many forms. What they all have in common is that they create an environment where members are exposed to consistent negativity and psychological harm. Employees in a toxic workplace often lack autonomy, job security, and job satisfaction, receive little to no support from leadership, and have a high workload for which they're given inadequate compensation and recognition. The prevalence of toxic workplaces varies depending on the industry, but it is a pervasive issue—and reports of toxicity are consistently on the rise.

What causes toxicity in organization cultures, how can you differentiate a toxic workplace from a demanding one—and, if you're in one, is there any way to change it? We'll tackle each of those questions over the next three chapters. To start, let's dig deeper into what toxicity actually means and looks like in the real world.

What Exactly Is Toxicity?

The Meriam Webster definition of toxic is "very harmful or unpleasant in a pervasive or insidious way," and this is a good working definition. An environment that's toxic could be harmful and unpleasant in a physical way, like a build-up of carbon dioxide in a mine or the lingering radioactivity around Chernobyl. Environments can also be psychologically toxic when they cause pervasive, insidious feelings of anxiety, depression, frustration, or hopelessness in those who experience them. This kind of toxicity can still cause physical harm, too, leading to stress-related ailments like insomnia, chronic head and body aches, and immune system impairment that negatively impact the quality of life for the affected individual.

While workplaces can be physically toxic, in most cases members are dealing with the psychological form. A toxic workplace is one in which individual members feel personally threatened and lack a sense of psychological safety. This isn't the same thing as a workplace that's stressful or demanding. Someone can have a difficult job but still feel respected, valued, and safe when they're at work. Differentiating between a hard workplace and a toxic workplace in the real world can be challenging (we'll go into more depth on spotting the signs of toxicity in the next chapter), but as a general rule they're similar to the behavior seen in abusive inter-personal relationships, and can have a similarly damaging impact on the physical and mental health of victims. This includes a lack of control over your work environment, a lack of physical or emotional boundaries, belittling or demeaning treatment from coworkers or supervisors, and being harassed, bullied, or sabotaged in the workplace. Other common toxic behaviors include harmful gossip, ostracization or exclusion, and emotional outbursts in the workplace. A boss who regularly screams at reports and storms around the office slamming doors isn't just passionate or demanding, however they justify their behavior. Like abusers, the perpetrators of toxicity abdicate responsibility for their behavior and the harm it causes. A coworker who sabotages your work may rationalize it as normal workplace competition, or deflect blame back onto you for the failure. Another example would be a boss who regularly insults his reports but insists he's only teasing them or making a joke when called out—again, often flipping the blame to say the offended employee should learn how to take a joke or have a thicker skin.

The increase in remote work may seem like a godsend to those stuck in toxic workplaces, but while physical distance can dull the impact of some toxic behaviors it doesn't eradicate them. In some cases, toxicity gets worse in a remote setting. The added distance also decreases empathy and gives interactions a veil of anonymity, leading people to say thoughtless, hurtful, or offensive things they wouldn't say in person. Those who work from home are more isolated from coworkers than in an office setting, with fewer opportunities for social interaction that can build allies and support networks.

Similar to victims in abusive relationships, the employees in a toxic workplace often suffer in silence. Toxic behaviors like gaslighting make the victim question their perception of the situation, making them more hesitant to share their experience. When the toxicity stems from leadership, workers may fear retribution if they speak up about their treatment, and often don't know who they can trust or confide in. Other times, the victim loses perspective and internalizes the toxicity, coming to believe they deserve the treatment they're getting or rationalizing the behavior as normal or "just the way things are done here." This is how toxicity becomes systemic in organizations. Because the victim has convinced themselves their treatment was justified, they behave the same way to new hires or reports as they move up the ladder, entrenching the toxicity into the organization's culture.

Systemic toxicity can develop in any type of work place, but it's a more widespread problem in some industries than others. Workers at most risk for experiencing a toxic environment are at-will employees in minimum wage or low-wage positions, particularly those in fast-paced and/or low-margin industries. Consumer services businesses, like food service and hospitality, are at elevated risk for toxicity, as are creative industries like film production, video game design, and marketing. Tech startups are also prone to developing toxic habits when they lose sight of worker needs and limitations in their drive to innovate. Newcomers to these workplaces are often expected to "pay their dues" by working long or unusual hours for little pay, often while being disrespected, ignored, insulted, or abused by coworkers and managers. Individuals who speak up or push back are chased out; those who stick around internalize the culture as a kind of rite of passage that must be endured to advance. These environments are difficult to change because the ones who stick around have stopped seeing the culture as the problem. Instead, the ones who leave are seen as weak; enduring the toxicity is seen as proof of their strength and worth, often taken as a point of professional pride. Rooting out the toxicity means shifting the mindset of members at all levels. The overwhelming scope of that task is what stops many from even trying.

What Causes Toxicity in the Workplace?
The behaviors mentioned above aren't just the signs of toxicity. They're also what generates it. A person feels psychologically unsafe when they've experienced something hurtful or negative in that space. This can happen in any type of interaction: from the top down (e.g. a manager screaming at an employee for a minor mistake), from the bottom up (e.g. an employee spreading hurtful rumors about their manager), from peers (e.g. constant criticism from a coworker), or from external sources (e.g. repeated interactions with an abusive customer).

In the majority of toxic environments, the problem starts at the top. How leaders act and speak establishes the code of conduct for the organization. When they're hostile or disrespectful, that teaches other members this is acceptable behavior. A lack of leadership can be just as damaging. Poor communication, inconsistent enforcement of rules, and unclear workplace expectations confuse employees and makes their job stressful. People who are under stress have a harder time controlling their emotions and are more likely to say or do things before thinking through them clearly. Absent or inattentive leaders can't spot the signs of bullying, discrimination, or harassment, putting the responsibility on victims and coworkers to report it—but they're less likely to do so if they think the manager doesn't care. In these cases, the direct source of toxicity may be an individual contributor, but the environment that allowed them to thrive was created by leadership.

In a certain sense, you can think of toxicity like a fungus. Mold grows in neglected spaces because they provide the perfect conditions for it to thrive. Preventing this environment requires regular maintenance, sealing up cracks as they form before moisture can seep in. If you create a space that's dry, warm, and well-lit, the mold spores will die before they can bloom. In a workplace, an unhealthy employee environment creates conflict, hostility, distrust, and resentment, and that's a fertile breeding ground for toxic behavior.

Toxic behavior isn't always rooted in hostility. In some cases, it's caused more by ignorance than intent. This often happens when people are put into leadership positions without being given proper training on the people management side of the job. As a result, they may violate employee boundaries or set unrealistic expectations in the name of high standards without realizing the negative impact on their team. Insufficient training also leaves these leaders ill-equipped to solve issues and deal with crises, leading to managers who are apologetically toxic; they don't want to call their team in every Saturday, but they don't know how to manage the workload better to avoid it. When these poorly prepared managers fail to deliver results, they're more likely to exhibit behaviors like deflecting blame or kicked dog syndrome.

Along with these consistent sources of toxicity, there are a few likely factors in its current upward trend. Uncivil behavior in general is on the rise, especially in the workplace. Christine Porath and Christine Pearson, professors at Arizona State University's Thunderbird School of Global Management, conducted a long-term study of

14,000 professionals across industries. In 2011, 98% of respondents said they'd experienced incivility in their workplace, about half reporting experiencing it at least once a week, an increase of 25% over answers the pair received in 1998. Technology plays a role in this. The growing prevalence of online interactions makes people less mindful of how they interact with others because they can't immediately see the impact of their words and actions on the other person. Increased connectivity makes 24/7 communication possible, leading to overwhelmed, burned-out employees when managers take advantage of this to send work communications during their off-time. Consumers expect to receive goods and services faster today than they did in the past, adding to the pressure for companies to deliver fast results, often at the expense of employee health.

The power dynamic between management and employees has shifted over the past few decades, and this is likely another factor in the rise of toxic workplaces. In 1983, roughly 20% of the United States workforce belonged to a union. By 2020, the union membership rate had dropped to 10.8%. This decrease in collective bargaining power means employees are on their own when they report issues, with no one to advocate on their behalf when they're mistreated or taken advantage of by leadership. Accompanying this has been a gradual erosion of worker protections and social safety nets, making workers feel trapped in harmful work environments and unscrupulous leaders feel they can exploit workers without repercussions.

Consequences of a Toxic Environment
Anyone who's worked in a toxic environment is painfully aware of how it can impact individuals within the organization. Living with the day-to-day anxiety and stress of a hostile workplace damages both

your physical and mental health, and there's data to prove it. Research conducted by the University of South Australia in 2021 shows employees in toxic workplaces are three times more likely to suffer from depression, while a systematic meta-analysis published in *The Lancet* in 2015 found a correlation between high work stress and increased risk of heart disease and stroke. Particularly, those who worked long hours were 5 times more likely develop coronary heart disease and 10 times more likely to suffer a stroke than those who worked standard hours (30-40 per week).

The health impacts of toxic workplaces are likely a factor in another consequence of a toxic workplace: employees quit more often. As Wharton professor Nancy Rothbard says, a toxic work environment puts "corrosive pressures" on employees, "and these corrosive pressures are draining them and making them want to leave." In the Society for Human Resource Management's 2019 Culture Report, 58% of employees who left a job because of its culture did so because of a manager's behavior. They estimated the cost of turnover from toxicity to business at $223 billion over the 5-year span from 2014-2019. In the Porath and Pearson surveys mentioned above, nearly half of those who experienced incivility in the workplace intentionally spent less time at work after, and 12% quit because of it. Even if employees don't quit a toxic workplace, they're rarely able (or willing) to do their best work. Among respondents to the Porath and Pearson survey who stayed in their job after experiencing incivility, 78% said they felt less committed to the organization, 48% intentionally gave less effort at work, 38% intentionally lowered the quality of their work, and 25% said they'd taken their frustrations out on customers.

This drop in work quality may not be intentional, either. A study by Amir Erez, a professor of management at the University of Florida, found that experiencing or witnessing rude behavior negatively impacts a person's ability to think critically and creatively. Across his study, those who were treated rudely before being asked to solve problems produced about 25% fewer overall solutions, and the solutions they did give were less creative. Simply observing rude or hostile behavior can negatively impair our cognitive ability. In one experiment, participants were asked to complete a word puzzle after witnessing rude behavior. They performed on average 20% worse than members of the control group who hadn't watched the negative interaction.

It doesn't take study data for to know that conflict makes people uncomfortable. If you've ever been the third wheel to an argument, you know how awkward it feels to watch two people fight, or see someone get reprimanded in public. This adds another motivation to eliminate toxicity for customer-facing businesses. When a workplace is unhealthy, those conflicts don't always stay behind the scenes. A store where the staff is always arguing, or where the workers always seem to be in a bad mood, isn't a place anybody wants to spend their time as an employee or a patron.

Toxicity in Today's Workplace

There is a potential positive hidden in the rising rate of workplace toxicity. While toxic behavior does seem to be increasing, the numbers are likely inflated by a corresponding increase in awareness about what toxicity looks like and why it's damaging to organizations. Current labor trends suggest the pendulum of power may be shifting direction, with a growing push for stronger protections and more control for workers in shaping their work environment. This has empowered more employees to seek out a healthier workplace, or feel safe speaking up about the negative treatment they've experienced.

Empowerment and safety are the keywords when you're detoxifying an organization. Members who are afraid of losing their job if they stand up for themselves, or who have given up hope that the environment will change, are unlikely to report future toxic behaviors they witness or experience. The longer it continues in the shadows, the harder it is to identify and eliminate the sources of toxicity in your organization.

Chapter 2

SIGNS OF A TOXIC WORKPLACE ENVIRONMENT

Toxicity in a workplace environment is often something that's easier to feel than to define. Those who work within it on a day-to-day basis know it's toxic because they feel anxious, afraid, ignored, or disrespected when they're in the workplace. One of the most insidious issues with a toxic environment is that these individuals may not feel empowered to share these feelings, however. This means those on the outside can't count on first-hand accounts as an accurate way to detect toxicity, particularly those in leadership who are disconnected from the day-to-day culture, or members who are part of the majority community who want to be advocates for colleagues from under-represented groups.

There are a variety of ways that toxicity can manifest within a workplace—and, unfortunately, even the best-intentioned organization has the potential to become toxic. While toxicity often comes from upper leadership, it can originate at any level of the organization, and it can be equally damaging to the culture and well-being of the team whether it comes from individual contributors, middle managers, or upper leadership. Luckily, members at all levels also have the power to spot and solve toxicity. The first step to doing so is knowing what to look out for, and what those signs indicate about your organization as a whole.

Types of Toxic Cultures

What do you picture when you think of a toxic work environment? Most will probably conjure an image of an angry boss, who slams doors and screams at employees over small mistakes. Or perhaps you picture extreme bias, where sexual harassment and race-based discrimination are built into the status quo. While these are both definitely examples of toxicity, it doesn't always take such an obvious form. This can, in fact, be part of the problem in rooting out more subtle issues with the workplace culture. Employees only associate toxicity with almost cartoonishly extreme archetypes of the "bad boss" or "terrible coworker", and this makes them blind to the other ways disfunction and negativity can spread through an organization.

Even in businesses with an intentionally created culture, much of the day-to-day work environment is built through the interpersonal interactions of employees and leadership—and, as with anything involving human beings, that makes it inherently complicated. While each workplace is unique, however, there are some universal signs that there's a problem in your organizational environment, such as:

- **High turnover.** When employees can't please the boss, never get recognition, and lack control over their career path and work/life balance, they won't want to work in that environment long. Add in the employees that are chased out because of bias or overly harsh standards, and you end up with an unsustainable level of turnover in many toxic workplaces.

- **Poor communication.** Management may be unclear or inconsistent about workplace expectations, and employees often struggle to get feedback on their performance. This goes the other way, too—if leadership is uninterested in or unresponsive to employee feedback, that's a likely sign of toxicity.

- **Frequent employee burnout.** Overwork, lack of boundaries, and elevated levels of workplace stress are the most common contributing factors to burnout. When this happens on a regular basis, that's a sign something's wrong with the workplace, not an indictment of the individual employees' strength and abilities.

- **Low accountability.** A "not my job" attitude is a bad sign in any workplace, and especially so when it comes from the leadership level. If individuals in your organization are more concerned with assigning blame than solving problems, that's a sign of a problem.

- **Unequal or nonexistent employee recognition.** The standards for exceptional work should be clear and achievable for all employees—and, when they reach them, all employees should be equally lauded. Lack of recognition, or inconsistent recognition, leads to resentment and disengagement, and often stems from a deeper source of toxicity.

- **Lack of employee autonomy.** When employees feel managers are constantly looking over their shoulder, or have their work controlled down to every minute detail, this erodes workplace trust and increases employee anxiety, creating a workplace that's unhealthy.

Does this sound familiar? If so, there's a good chance your workplace is operating under one of the following toxic cultures:

Authoritative Culture

This is the environment that springs to mind first when most people hear the words "workplace toxicity." In this type of workplace, authority is derived from control, and bullying, abuse, and discrimination are common. This bullying usually starts with upper leadership, who aggressively assert their hierarchical authority to the detriment of individual contributors. Transparency is often non-existent; leaders may withhold knowledge from employees, and rarely listen to feedback or ideas from employees. Those who share dissenting opinions, or speak up about workplace problems, are ignored or silenced, and may be punished for their honesty, or passed over for advancement opportunities under the justification that they're "not a team player."

This type of behavior from upper leadership has a ripple effect through the organization. Ambitious employees learn the best way to get ahead is to agree with the boss, or to bully and undermine their colleagues to make themselves look better. The favoritism and nepotism that run rampant in these cultures means only "yes-men" are able to survive and thrive, leaving those who want to change the culture no allies to turn to among management and senior staff. Since only those who agree with leadership are given a voice in the workplace, employees who are bullied or discriminated against have no recourse, often driving them to find employment elsewhere.

Hustle Culture

This is one of the most normalized forms of workplace toxicity, and is especially common in tech startups and profit-driven corporate environments. Workaholism is glamorized to the point that it becomes the standard. Employees are expected to put in extra hours, whether in the office or working from home, and feel guilty when they take breaks or use their PTO; those who dare to end their shifts on time or refuse overtime are seen as weak, lazy, or lacking dedication. Even when employees are off the clock, managers may expect them to respond to work-related communications, giving them the feeling they can never sign off or stop thinking about work completely.

Hustle cultures often form when the leadership lacks empathy and has micromanagement tendencies. Management is concerned only with results and maximizing productivity, and is willing to overwork team members to the point of burnout to reach them. In the interest of cutting costs, they may delay filling open positions, instead assigning that work to the remaining staff and forcing them to work even more, exacerbating the problem. This is ultimately short-sighted, ignoring the long-term costs and productivity drop that comes when employees reach their breaking point. Hustle cultures also often form in creative industries, especially those with tight deadlines like video game production, exploiting employees' passion for their work to get them to agree to extreme hours or a lack of work/life balance.

<u>Disjointed Culture</u>

In a healthy workplace, the company's stated core values align with their day-to-day operations, decision-making process, and member behavior standards. When this doesn't happen, the culture becomes disjointed. This leaves employees guessing about how they're supposed to behave in the workplace, and leaves it up to individual managers how they'll interpret and enforce policies, opening the door for favoritism and other individual biases.

Like authoritative cultures, disjointed cultures often suffer from a lack of transparency and poor communication, as well as toxic behaviors like yelling, gossip, and bullying. The difference is these behaviors don't always come from the top down. Instead, upper management is often distant or lacks a clear vision, allowing bullies and other bad apples at lower hierarchy levels to poison the culture.

Blame Culture

In this workplace, employees don't feel supported by their managers and there's an unhealthy feeling of competition between coworkers, rather than a spirit of collaboration. This often starts from leaders who won't take accountability for their mistakes, setting a precedent that gets ingrained into the culture. It can also arise at the team member level in response to overly harsh or micromanaging leaders. Whatever the cause, employees are afraid to lose status (or their jobs) by owning up to their own mistakes. They also may resist learning new skills, taking on big projects, or committing to deadlines, impeding their career progress and the growth of the team as a whole.

Clique Culture

People will naturally form closer friendships with some coworkers than others in a healthy workplace. Cliques happen when these groupings affect work-related activities. Very often, clique culture intersects with bias and discrimination, such as the "boys club" culture in fields like law, finance, and tech that have been historically male-dominated. When cliques form in a workplace, this undermines the team dynamic and breaks down the trust bonds between coworkers, leading to back-stabbing, knowledge-hoarding, rumor-spreading, and other disruptive, distracting behaviors. If one clique is dominant, those who don't fit in often feel they can't be their authentic selves in the workplace. They may be left out of meetings, projects, and social outings, leaving them feeling invisible and isolated and, in many cases, driving them to look for a new job.

Cliques are able to form in a workplace when the leadership is inattentive and fails to commit fully to creating an inclusive culture. Management ignores or downplays inappropriate or offensive jokes, comments, and actions, sending the message that it's okay to treat people differently depending on what group they belong to. When those cliques also include members of leadership, the situation can become even more toxic for those from non-majority groups, allowing for discrimination to become systemic and affect the organization at the policy level.

Fear-based Culture

A fear-based environment is one of the most toxic workplace cultures, and the one likely to have the most negative impact on both the organization and individuals within it. In these cultures, authority is derived from intimidation or harsh enforcement of the rules. It's a culture of "the stick without the carrot", where threat of punishment is the main tactic to drive productivity. Other abusive behaviors, like gaslighting and public shaming, are also often employed to keep employees from questioning the harsh treatment of leadership.

Employees in these cultures often exist in a state of constant anxiety, and will do whatever it takes to avoid punishment, including passing blame, cutting corners, and other unproductive behavior. These workplaces also often have an active rumor mill as employees desperately try to predict what management will do next and how they can avoid becoming the next target of their abuse.

Identifying Toxic Leaders

You probably noticed a consistent theme in all the types of toxic cultures described in the last section: all of them can (and often are) originate with leadership. While it's true that toxicity can come from anywhere in an organization, those who make decisions and write policies have the most power over the culture. To put it another way, a toxic culture can form under a reasonable leader, but it's nearly impossible to maintain a healthy culture with a toxic leader at the helm.

Just because a leader is demanding doesn't mean they're toxic. It's fine for a manager to have high expectations for their team, so long as those expectations are made clear from the outset, applied equally to every member, and team members are rewarded when they meet them. So what does indicate leadership toxicity? Here are some common signs to look out for:

- **Narcissism.** A narcissistic leader only thinks about themselves, rather than focusing on the needs of the team. Often, they exhibit a lack of both empathy and self-awareness, making them blind to how their behavior affects their team.
- **Favoritism.** An effective leader gives accolades, promotions, and other rewards based on actions, not unearned privilege. The same is true on the discipline side of the equation. Inequal enforcement of rules and distribution of opportunities is one of the most common forms of leadership toxicity.
- **Ignoring employee input.** It's not always possible for managers to act on every suggestion or complaint from employees—but they can (and should) make a concerted effort. A manager who consistently ignores their reports likely doesn't prioritize them when making decisions, either.

- **Emotional outbursts.** The leaders of an organization should be the metaphorical adults in the room. It's obviously toxic when bosses throw tantrums, scream, and slam doors, but more subtle forms of emotional manipulation, like guilt trips or public breakdowns, are equally inappropriate.

- **Unrealistic expectations.** There is a fine line between demanding excellence and asking for the impossible. When managers set unrealistic deadlines, it forces employees to choose between sacrificing their work quality, or sacrificing their quality of life—an unfair thing to ask any employee.

- **Low emotional IQ.** Bad bosses often seem to forget their reports are human. This lack of compassion stems from a low emotional IQ, and leads to them ignoring the psychological and emotional health of their team so long as they're achieving their desired results.

- **Micromanagement.** It's healthy for a boss to be hands-on and communicative with their team. Micromanagement happens when the leader needs to be involved in every small decision. If the manager doesn't trust their hires to make day-to-day decisions, the company can't move forward.

- **Dishonesty or withholding information.** Honesty is necessary to build trust. When employees feel they can't trust their manager, this infects the entire culture.

- **Irregular or inconsistent feedback.** On a similar vein, employees should know their manager's expectations and be able to find out where they stand. Absent leadership and a lack of leader input can be just as damaging to a culture as overtly toxic behavior.

- **Credit stealing.** It's one thing to celebrate group accomplishments, or share the credit for a job well done between members of the team. Toxic bosses take all that credit for themselves, regardless of their actual role in the work.

- **Retaliatory discipline.** Disciplinary action should be corrective, not punitive. Toxic bosses will often use their authority in selfish, unproductive ways, and this includes doling out reprimands or write-ups out of anger or revenge.

It's well-documented that a bad boss can wreak havoc on an organization. According to a survey from Harvard Business School, 57% of employees who quit do so because of a bad manager. Customers or clients who witness a boss' bad behavior may also be driven away, causing damage to the entire company's reputation that can be very difficult to repair. If managers in your organization show any of the signs above, it's time to do some soul searching as a leadership team.

Employee-level Toxicity

A toxic employee could be generally described as anyone whose behavior is disruptive or harmful to the organization. While they may not have as much of an impact on the organization as a toxic leader, anyone who's worked with a toxic colleague can attest to the damage they cause on the team level. In many cases, toxic employees don't exist in a vacuum. Some of the most common bad workplace behaviors arise in response to indifference, bullying, or other unhealthy behaviors from leadership. This is why it's smart to look for signs of toxicity from the top down.

Astute managers can weed out potentially toxic employees in the interview stage by asking the right questions and paying attention to their body language and other nonverbal clues (we'll share more tips on doing that later in the book). That said, these employees are often manipulative, and may present an ideal self in the interview, only showing their true colors once they've settled in to the workplace. They often have very high self esteem, giving them a confidence that's perceived as correctness and charisma, another reason they can be so tricky to identify and deal with from the coworker level. Even if they're high individual performers, however, these toxic employees are harmful to the team dynamic. They bring out the worst in their team members, fostering negativity and taking advantage of the misfortunes of others to serve their own gains. This is why it's worth the effort to stop this behavior or remove the employee, even if they're one of your top performers—it's possible they're always at the front of the pack because they've pushed everybody else down on their way there.

Like with toxic work environments, there are different types of toxic employees. Some of the most common:

- **The bulldozer.** These employees plow over their coworker's ideas and opinions in their quest to get their way. They're often loud, aggressive, and frequently interrupt others when they're speaking. They also often argue with what others say, and feel that they're always right (and others are wrong, if they disagree).
- **The gossiper.** It's natural to talk a bit about your coworkers, but those employees who seem to always have a new rumor to share are at best a distraction, and can be actively harmful to their colleagues if they share confidential information about them, or spread untrue rumors meant to disrupt their work relationships.
- **The knowledge hoarder.** Transparency and honesty are how trust bonds are built in a workplace, and knowledge hoarders

disrupt this balance. Their actions usually arise out of fear: in order to maintain their job security, they make themselves the only ones with a certain skill set or knowledge, refusing to train or inform colleagues. This can create a task bottleneck that makes your workplace less efficient, and is an even bigger problem if they quit, since you won't be left with anyone who can fill their shoes.

- **The oversharer.** This is similar to the gossiper except they don't talk about other people as often as they air their own dirty laundry. These individuals create drama by bringing their personal problems into the workplace, distracting their colleagues and creating an unpleasant environment anytime they're in the office.

- **The credit stealer/the under-performer.** Those who take credit for the work of others don't always do it obviously. In some cases, they're so charismatic and well-liked by coworkers that they become a magnet for weaker personalities, who gravitate toward them and gladly pick up the credit-stealer's slack, while allowing them to take credit for the effort.

- **The complainer.** There's a difference between a bit of healthy venting between peers, and someone who constantly has something to complain about. Even if the source of their complaints is valid, their way of expressing those issues is off—they're talking to the wrong people, often, or not willing to put in the effort to make real changes. As a result, their "woe is me" attitude creates a pervasive negativity within the workplace.

- **The know-it-all.** Similar to the bulldozer, these individuals are quick to brag about their accomplishments and insist they have all the knowledge and information (even when they clearly don't). They also tend to be resistant to criticism and slow to apologize when they do realize they were wrong.

- **The passive-aggressive.** These individuals avoid conflict to a fault. Rather than speaking up when they have an issue, they'll bottle their feelings, redirecting them into backhand comments, snippy remarks, and procrastination of work they don't want to do.

Can a Remote Workplace be Toxic?

In some ways, the shift to remote work was a godsend for employees stuck in toxic work environments, providing an extra layer of distance between them and bullies, bad bosses, and other sources of toxicity. Unfortunately, going remote doesn't eliminate the chance of a toxic workplace entirely. There are subtle, pervasive ways a remote environment can be toxic, and they're often more difficult to identify than in physical workspaces because of the potential for private interactions.

Many of the signs of remote toxicity are similar to those for other toxic work environments. The biggest sign is that team members are overworked, underpaid, and underappreciated. Remote workers are more likely to be passed over for raises and promotions, while working from home makes it all too easy for work time to bleed over into the evenings and weekends, creating an environment where you can never sign off. Making matters worse, leadership may feel these individuals don't need vacations, or expect them to continue working through PTO because they have a remote framework to do so. In some cases, job responsibilities or roles may have shifted with the change to remote work, but that information was never conveyed properly to the ones doing the job, leaving expectations vague and generating resentment if the employee's being asked to do more for the same pay.

A lack of a viable communication system for remote workers is the biggest sign of a toxic remote environment. Remote employees may be left out of meetings and other activities, or not told about major changes or big projects that are only discussed within the office. Going along with this, remote employees get fewer chances for recognition and rewards, and may be denied raises or promotions, or have no clearly outlined path for advancement within the company. If the entire senior leadership team works in person, this is a likely sign remote workers aren't given the consideration they're due—the only way for one to be added to that inner circle would be for them to give up their remote work. On the other side of things are remote workers subjected to micromanagement, such as bosses who demand needless screenshots, use of time tracking apps, and other oversight they don't expect from in-person workers.

The shift to a digital workspace requires more than just a few extra programs. It requires that managers refine they way they lead teams, evaluate work progress, and manage communication. If your company leapt into remote work without a solid plan in place, odds are they haven't fully thought through what a remote workplace should look like, and that means an equitable, healthy workplace can only happen by chance.

Identifying Toxicity Across Levels

Toxicity has become a buzzword, but at its root it's quite simple. Any behavior that creates an uncomfortable, hostile, or disrespectful work environment for some or all of your employees is toxic, whether it's coming from the upper leadership or the newest entry-level hire. While senior leadership has the most control to change the culture, they're also often the last ones to identify the problem;

the employees who live it everyday can't ignore it, and many will be driven away as a result.

In a ResumeLab survey of employees from a range of industries, 72% of respondents said they'd been treated rudely by a bad boss. About 70% had been criticized in front of peers, while 42% witnessed their boss blaming others for their failures. These statistics highlight how severe of a problem workplace toxicity is. So what can you do about it? We'll discuss that in the next chapter.

Chapter 3:

DE-TOXIFYING YOUR WORKPLACE

The statistics on toxicity are alarming. Roughly 40% of people have been bullied at work, according to research by Mental Health America, and nearly half of those report suffering health problems after as a result of the stress. Many of these people don't report their mistreatment, either out of fear of retaliation or because they feel it's pointless to do so. When it is reported, too often it's dismissed by leaders as employees being over-sensitive to a demanding leadership style.

All of this can sometimes make the situation feel hopeless, especially for those who are trying to fix toxicity from the employee or middle management level. It's true that those at the top have the most agency for addressing problems with the culture, but that's not to say those lower in the hierarchy are powerless to make change. If you've spotted the signs of toxicity outlined in the last chapter, there are certainly steps you can take to improve the work environment for yourself and others.

From Leadership: Steps for Fixing a Toxic Culture

Bad behavior in the workplace doesn't happen in a vacuum. Even when employees are the ones actively perpetuating a negative culture, it's a failure of leadership that allows them to do so. These bad apples can only spoil the barrel because leadership fails to address and remove them, whether due to ignorance, indifference, or their own toxic inclinations. The bottom line is, team members learn what's acceptable in the workplace from those at the top. If they're engaging in offensive or harmful behavior, it's either because they don't know their actions are wrong or because they believe they can get away with it based on their observations of others' words and actions. Either way, that's something leadership has the most power to address.

Changing a negative culture can be a long and arduous process, and more so when those issues are long-rooted and woven into the structure and policies of the organization. Change is possible, though, even for the most toxic workplaces. Here are some solid steps you can take to make meaningful, lasting improvements to your culture.

Step 1: Open a dialogue with employees.
Acknowledging that there's a problem—and determining exactly what issues are plaguing your workplace—is the first step. Those at the employee level are likely to have more insights into this than leadership, who are often isolated from the effects of toxicity. Open two-way communication can open your eyes to what's going on under your nose, at the same time giving employees a chance to voice their concerns about behavior they've observed or experienced at work.

Keep in mind that it may take some time and effort to get your employees to open up. Team members won't be completely honest if they're afraid that reporting the behavior of managers or well-liked colleagues will result in punishment or impact their own career progress. In these cases, a mix of anonymous surveys, one-on-one conversations, and group discussions will be necessary to fully identify the problems that need to be addressed. You also don't want this feedback to be a one-and-done situation. Whatever communication system you put in place, make sure you have a process for regular reporting of bullying, harassment, discrimination, or other negative behaviors that happen in the future.

<u>Step 2: Review your data, policies, and behavior.</u>
In some cases, toxicity arises from individuals in the organization. More often, though, the issues with the culture are systemic, and it will take more than a few corrective actions of bad apples to truly get to the root of the issue. Look at all the information you've collected, both testimonials from employees and figures like turnover, pay rates, and engagement.

Don't assume you as the leader are exempt from these issues, either. Part of this review process should be an analysis of your own behavior as a leader and taking responsibility for your role in the organization's problems. Think about how you interact with your team members when you're under pressure—do you take it out on them by shouting or throwing fits? How often do you recognize your employees' strong work, and when you do, is it based on observed actions, or do promotions and raises go to the people you like? When employees report issues, do you respond defensively, or do you listen to their concerns and act on them? In some cases, leaders can make well-intentioned missteps, like avoiding confrontation with a problematic employee out of a desire to keep the peace. Be honest with yourself, and take any criticisms you're given seriously, even if you don't agree with them. If you struggle to perform this kind of self-analysis, consider bringing in a consultant who can observe your workplace interactions impartially with fresh eyes.

<u>Step 3: Revise policies to re-establish a sense of safety.</u>
Policies don't need to be actively harmful to contribute to workplace toxicity. In some cases, it's a lack of clear policies that allows these issues to grow and persist. As a leader, you have the power to re-write and re-establish those guidelines to make sure everyone knows exactly what is and isn't acceptable behavior in your workplace. Use the information you've collected to guide this process, and don't ignore or downplay the concerns expressed by your team. Doing so amounts to an institutional betrayal, and will make them less likely to speak up about issues they experience in the future.

Once you've clarified expectations and revised your policies, communicate these changes loudly and publicly. You need to re-assure victimized employees that they have a voice and things are actually going to improve to get everyone on board. Whatever toxic behaviors have been allowed in the past, the perpetrators need to know they won't be tolerated in the future. This includes issues that prevent employees from maintaining a healthy work/life balance, like expectations of working "off the clock" after employee shifts should have ended, or managers who regularly communicate with employees on their off days. Ultimately, the goal is a workplace where all individuals are seen as both valuable contributors and actual human beings, not just for what they contribute to the bottom line. Ensure future communications are conducted respectfully and that two-way conversation stays open as you move forward. In some cases, this may mean providing additional training to managers or employees to make sure they understand the new standards of behavior.

<u>Step 4: Reward good behavior (and correct the bad).</u>

Follow-up is key when you're correcting culture problems. Those employees who are accustomed to being ignored or excluded may carry some trauma from that experience even after the policies have been corrected, and will need help healing and learning to trust the organization again. Be proactive in recognizing individual and team achievements to make sure everyone on the team feels like they belong there. On the other end, those who have been allowed to make offensive comments in the past may need reminders that this is no longer acceptable. Be firm in correcting their behavior, even if that means disciplining individuals that you had thought of before as your best employees. This carrot-and-stick approach is nothing revolutionary, but it works.

As you move forward, make sure you continue to observe the interactions of coworkers, especially those who are brought onboard after these policy changes took place. Pay attention to how people interact and keep an eye out for individuals who dominate conversations, or those who are regularly excluded, talked over, or undermined. For these changes to truly have an effect you need everyone to be onboard, or else future victims will fall into the same pattern of suffering in silence that allowed the toxicity to take root in the first place.

Can Middle Managers Fix a Toxic Culture?

For middle managers, it's easy to feel stuck and powerless—and, again, this tends to be the case most often in toxic workplaces, where there isn't enough communication and transparency, and no one but the upper management are able to enact policy changes. If you have an oblivious or abusive CEO, there's often little you can do from below to "manage up" and change their behavior. There are steps you can take to protect your team members from their influence, though, and sometimes small changes from the middle-management level can have a huge impact on the day-to-day lives of your reports.

Like with upper leadership, the first step is to take a close look at your own behavior. Don't pass along the disrespect of upper leaders to your team members, and make sure that you're giving recognition to your team when they deserve it and listening to their concerns. When you're facing pressures from both sides, it can sometimes be easy to get lost in the shuffle and forget to give employees the acknowledgment they deserve. While this is understandable, though, it doesn't make it excusable. Part of being a leader of people is acknowledging their needs as human beings. Pay attention to your team's mental health and keep an eye out for those who are struggling. Learn to recognize the signs and symptoms of anxiety, burnout, and depression, so you can intervene and find out what needs to change when you see them among reports. Part of this stems back to what the team thinks your expectations are. If you reward people who sacrifice their mental health or work/life balance for the team, this will seem like the only way to get ahead in your company. Instead, encourage those who work overtime to stop when their shift is over, or take advantage of their paid time off, and make it clear that you, at least, don't expect anyone to give up their health and happiness for the sake of the company.

Keep in mind, too, that you don't need to be part of the C-level to implement new systems or processes. While you may not have the power to change the organization's rules, managers at any level can create a feedback system to gain deeper insights into how the team is doing and empower them to report issues and concerns.

You also have the power to be transparent about your decisions, even if higher levels of the hierarchy don't do the same. When you're in the position to make decisions about promotions, raises, or team assignments, ensure you're doing so fairly and inclusively, and listen to team members when they feel you're failing to do so. Take a proactive approach to making these changes. Don't ask your bosses if you can let people leave when their shifts are over, or if your team is allowed to use their PTO; inform them that you will be encouraging them to do so and why, then make a point of reporting back on any positive changes to the morale that happen as a result. If they're against it and refuse then things may be out of your hand, but rather than waiting for approval, move ahead with these changes unless you explicitly are told no.

The amount of power and agency that middle managers has differs from one business to the next. Unfortunately, there are some organizations where those who aren't at the very top have little power to change the environment. If your own mental health is suffering as a result of this dynamic, it may be time for you to cut your losses and leave—and encourage your reports to do the same. Very often, good people get stuck at bad companies because they desperately want to improve the conditions, even when it's been proven time and time again that it's not possible. Remember, if you push too hard and burn yourself out you won't be able to help anyone. Do your best, but if that proves not to be enough, don't blame yourself. Everyone deserves a healthy workplace that respects their boundaries and values their contributions—and that includes those stuck in the middle.

Making Change from the Employee Level

If even middle managers are sometimes powerless to change a toxic environment, do employees have any hope at all of improving their lives and those of coworkers? The truth is, while it depends on the workplace, you may have more power than you think—and, as with middle management, the first step is to make sure you're part of the solution, not part of the problem. A toxic culture can lead well-intentioned and kind people to behave in ways they otherwise wouldn't. If you notice yourself picking up back habits as a result of working with rude, disrespectful, or discriminatory coworkers, take a step back and commit to breaking them.

Toxic cultures arise under ignorant or distant leaders as often as they do under hostile ones. Employees who bully or degrade their coworkers may act differently when leadership is around, preventing those in charge from seeing the full scope of the problem. Start your attempts at change by having a candid conversation with your manager or HR department. Explain the behavior you've observed, why it's a problem, and what you would like to have done about it. If you have data or other evidence to back up your claims, bring copies you can leave with them after the conversation. This isn't always an easy conversation to have, and more so for those who are in marginalized groups. Allies from the majority have the privilege of raising these concerns with less fear of reprisal, giving them extra power to be a driving force for change.

If leadership or HR responds negatively to your information—or doesn't respond at all—this doesn't mean you have no power. Find strength in numbers by forming a coalition with coworkers who share your concerns. Leadership and HR may be more receptive to your suggestions if they're brought by a team of many, preventing them from dismissing the problem as an isolated incident. Once you band together as a group, this opens up the opportunity to form a task force, employee resource group, or union that can organize the workforce and help prevent exploitation and discrimination in the future, or at the very least give those who are victims of it a recourse.

The Importance of Conversation

The connecting thread of the three sections above is awareness. Change starts by recognizing that toxicity exists within your organization, and identifying and changing your own behaviors that are contributing to the overall negativity. Those who are deeply enmeshed in the culture may not realize how toxic it truly is, especially if they've never experienced working in a healthy environment and don't have that context for comparison. It's important to remember that you can't speak toxicity into existence. Talking about the negative behavior you've experienced or witnessed in a constructive way lessens its influence and impact, and is absolutely crucial if you're going to find a way forward to a healthier culture.

Chapter 4:
BAD BOSSES

Here's a situation that might sound familiar. You land a job with a good company, doing work that gives you a lot of satisfaction, with a welcoming team of coworkers. Everything seems perfect—until you meet the boss. Maybe they're too demanding, contacting you at all hours of the night with unreasonable demands, or on the opposite end of the spectrum they seem to disappear just when you need them to answer a question or provide resources. Suddenly, that perfect job becomes something you dread, and you feel powerless to do anything about your situation.

The curse of the bad boss is unfortunately common in today's workplace. According to Employee Benefit News, 57% of employees who quit do so because of their boss. It also leads to disengagement, a phenomenon that costs businesses an estimated $450-$550 billion in losses each year according to a Gallup poll. This means that, while employees have the most immediate motivation to rectify a bad boss, it behooves companies to address the situation promptly, too.

Like toxic workplaces, bad bosses can take many forms, and are just as likely to damage the workplace culture as issues that occur at the organizational level. In some cases, employees can "manage up" to an ineffective boss to create a more amenable work environment.

Other times, though, the situation becomes untenable, and you're left with the unsavory choice of living with the situation or looking for a better one in another company or department. With all that in mind, let's take a look at some of the most common types of bad bosses and what employees can do to cope with their situation.

Abusive and Caustic Bosses

This is the archetype that will come to mind first for many when they hear the phrase "bad boss". These are the leaders who berate their employees over mistakes both large and small, even when they're in front of colleagues or customers. When a caustic boss is having a bad day, so is everyone else in the office. They take out their frustration and other negative emotions on the rest of the office, to the point employees may begin to dread seeing them open their office door.

An abusive boss' tirades may be generalized and directed at anyone who happens to be within shouting distance, or they may be targeted at a certain individual or group of people. This often intersects with other forms of discrimination and harassment, like racism and misogyny. Those who belong to the same tribe as the abusive boss may be spared from their worst behavior, while employees who come from marginalized groups are regularly subjected to rudeness, disrespect, belittling, and other forms of aggression.

<u>Dealing With Caustic Leaders</u>

The best approach to dealing with this type of boss depends on where they stand in the hierarchy. Approaching them directly is often a nonstarter, often only prompting a fresh tirade or making you an even more frequent target of their aggression. If they're a middle manager, or part of a broader upper leadership team, you may be able to go to

HR, or to the boss' boss and peers. Very often, leaders who are abusive with their reports behave more reasonably with those they see as equals or superiors, so others in leadership may not be aware of how harmful your boss' behavior is—and may even be grateful that you've shared this information with them. Prepare for this conversation by maintaining a log of the boss' abuse or harassment. Save any bullying texts, memos, or e-mails that you've received, as well as any other evidence you can provide. Check the laws for your state about audio recording, too, and if it's legal where you live buy a spy pen or other similar covert recording device that you can use to capture their next tirade. The more extensive the record of their behavior, the harder it will be to dismiss.

It's also a good idea to talk to others on your team who have been a victim of the boss' abuse. If nothing else you can commiserate and help each other know you're not alone, preventing the boss from gaslighting you into thinking their behavior is acceptable. A coalition often also has more success when reporting abusive behavior. The HR team may be tempted to brush off the report of a single worker as them being too sensitive (or even think that they did something to deserve it), but it's much harder to ignore or explain away similar statements from an entire team of individuals.

If the caustic boss is the sole or top leader—or if your report to HR or other leaders isn't taken seriously—there's unfortunately not much you can do to rectify this situation. In a larger company, you may be able to get out from under the boss' influence by switching to a different team or department. Otherwise, it's likely time to clean up your resume and get your ducks in a row to make a job switch.

Absent Bosses

An absent boss could be physically absent and unreachable—maybe they seem to always be on a vacation, or work out of a different building or floor and never bother to check in with their reports. This category also includes the "empty suit" archetype, who is physically present but functionally useless and unavailable. They may spend all their time in their office doing frivolous tasks, even when the rest of the team is overwhelmed with work, or fail to respond to questions, requests for approval, or other messages and tasks that only the boss can answer.

While absent bosses don't cause as much direct stress as caustic ones, they're still very demoralizing and difficult to work under. The lack of leadership and direction allows individuals to have too much influence over the culture and workplace, leading to the formation of cliques or de facto hierarchies that in turn lead to exclusion and bias. It's also simply a confusing workplace to be a part of since nobody really knows what the boss is thinking or expects at any given time. This often leads to mistakes and missed deadlines since employees aren't made aware of tasks in a timely manner, leading to unneeded stress and unhappy clients.

Dealing with Absent Leaders

If your job is just your job and you're not too concerned about making career progress, an absent boss may not be the worst thing in the world, especially if you're typically a more independent worker as it is. In this case, you can keep your head down, complete your tasks, collect your paycheck, and move on. For those who want to advance their careers with their company, however, it's a different story. If you don't know what's expected of you, and don't have anyone paying attention to your hard work, it's almost impossible to gain the recognition and opportunities that lead to future promotions.

Being proactive is the best option for employees who want to thrive under absent leaders. Take the initiative to organize your coworkers and communicate with clients to find out who is doing what and when it needs to be finished. If your immediate supervisor won't reply to your e-mails, reach out to their boss or another team leader to get the answers and guidance you need. While they're frustrating to work under, absent bosses can actually be an opportunity for ambitious employees to demonstrate their leadership abilities within the team.

Micromanagers

On the other end of the spectrum from bosses who are never around or involved in the day-to-day work are micromanagers: bosses who need to have their hands and eyes on every single little task that goes through their department. Often, they're so focused on the details of how tasks are completed that they fail to ensure the team produces the desired results. The need to constantly check in or respond to nagging messages slows down employees' work process, forcing them to work longer to achieve the same results. This type of leadership also erodes the trust between employees and management since employees feel the manager doesn't believe they know how to do the work correctly, ultimately increasing worker stress and killing engagement.

Micromanagement is harmful to an organization in other ways, too. Since employees aren't given agency to try their own ideas and work process, the company misses out on a lot of innovation and potential for growth. Employees are also much more likely to develop "learned helplessness" under a micromanager, where they assume they're not allowed to make any decisions without approval, losing their sense of empowerment and agency in the workplace.

<u>Dealing with Micromanagers</u>

While micromanagers can be frustrating to work under, at the very least you know what they want from you. In less egregious cases, the best option may just be to do things the way they want them done. It's at least worth it to try their approach—you may find it actually is the most efficient way, or if nothing else no worse than the way you'd prefer to work. Over time, as you demonstrate your ability to complete tasks on time to their satisfaction, they may grow to trust you and stop being quite so overbearing once you explain that you work better without such intense supervision.

Other micromanagers are the worst of both worlds: they want you to do things their way, but they don't communicate exactly what that way is, demanding that you redo projects and treating your work like it's never good enough, without clarifying exactly what they're looking for. In this case, a conversation with the micromanager is in order. Explain the issues that you're having and why it's negatively impacting your ability to work effectively. You're not going to be able to change their need to control every aspect of the workplace, but you can at least ask them for more insights about exactly what they're looking for so you don't have to waste time and effort guessing.

Incompetent Bosses

An incompetent boss can be one of the most frustrating to work under because they tend to actively generate problems that are beyond your control. Their specific issues can vary. In some cases, they may be so disorganized and flighty that you experience similar problems as with an absent boss, with tasks being assigned last-minute and few resources provided that will allow you to complete them correctly. Often, the result is you have to do two jobs: the one you've been hired to do, and the extra work of cleaning up after the manager and doing the work they won't or can't.

Incompetent bosses are also a massive time waster. They may schedule unnecessary meetings or fail to properly plan these conversations, making them last much longer than they need to. This lack of respect for other people's time rarely comes from a place of malice, but it's no less frustrating when you're on the receiving end. Other times, they may assign you meaningless work, or assign the same work to multiple team members, leading to duplicated efforts and confusion about who is working on what projects. Often, they have difficulty making firm decisions, or put decisions off until you need to rush to meet your deadline. In the worst cases, they may then pass the blame for this failing on to employees, refusing to acknowledge their role in creating the problems. However their incompetence manifests, the ultimate result is a dysfunctional workplace with low productivity and high levels of stress.

Dealing with an Incompetent Boss

Especially if the boss is young or new to management, this is the perfect situation for some up-managing from a more experienced report. Sit down with the manager privately and politely note the issues that you're seeing in the workplace, giving some suggestions of what would be more helpful for you and your colleagues. Take notes and document the instances where their indecision, lack of communication, unpreparedness, or other issues caused problems for the broader team and company, and give them some suggestions of what they could have done instead to lead to better outcomes. Not all managers will be open to this kind of inverse mentorship, but if it works it can greatly benefit your workplace and those who want to improve will be grateful for the insight, forging a connection that could benefit your career in the long term.

In the worst cases, when bosses are arrogant as well as incompetent, they won't respond as well to this kind of guidance. They may get defensive about you pointing out their failings or refuse to take your advice out of an assumption they know better because they have the hierarchical upper hand. You can sometimes still improve the situation by proactively implementing your own systems and organization, though other times the manager will take this as a slight or attack. If you're committed to the team, you may benefit from taking your documentation of their incompetence to upper leadership or HR. Otherwise, the best choice is often to find a team with a manager who has a better grasp of how to do their job.

Dishonest Bosses

Dishonesty from leadership can take many forms, and comes from an equally varied range of intentions. In some cases, it may come from a desire to avoid confrontation or delivering bad news. They may make grandiose promises that they know they can't keep because they don't want to disappoint their reports, or not want to give negative feedback because they don't want to hurt anyone's feelings. Other times, their dishonesty could stem from ego and selfishness. These managers see their reports as tools to improve their own image, telling them what they want to hear to keep them happy but freely discussing employee shortcomings with other leaders, or blaming them for problems when they occur. In the worst cases, the dishonest boss is intentionally manipulative, promising promotions or bonuses to lure employees to put in extra work then failing to deliver once the project's finished.

The truth is, it doesn't matter why the boss is dishonest. Whenever a manager promises something that doesn't materialize, lies to their employees, or fails to pass along necessary information, this erodes the trust in the employee/manager relationship. If this only happens rarely—and the manager owns up to their mistake and apologizes for it—that relationship can recover. The more common it is, though, the less likely employees will be to believe their next promise, and the more the culture will shift to one of resentment, cynicism, and general distrust.

<u>Dealing with Dishonest Bosses</u>

This is another situation where you may be able to do a bit of up-managing, especially if the manager's dishonesty is rooted in a genuine desire to keep their employees happy. Explain to the manager why it's actually helpful for their reports to receive negative feedback or hear bad news, and offer them some suggestions of ways they can deliver it that will soften the blow without avoiding the situation.

Intentionally dishonest mangers, on the other hand, are much more difficult to change or remove. For one thing, you have no idea what they've been telling the other leaders, who are unfortunately more likely to believe a peer than someone lower in the hierarchy. If you're working under an overtly manipulative manager, your best option is often to remove yourself from that situation.

Narcissistic Bosses

Narcissists by definition only care about themselves, seeing the people around them as means to an end for their own advancement or success.

This makes them poorly suited to manage other people, but they are often also charming and confident, traits that allow them to rise quickly through many corporate hierarchies. As leaders, they're not interested in coaching or supporting reports, and aren't interested in improving their happiness or work environment—or, if they are, it's with an ulterior motive.

Narcissistic managers are the most likely type to steal ideas from employees, take the credit for work done by reports, or act like they were solely responsible for team accomplishments. They also often engage in the manipulative behavior described above, saying one thing to reports and another to peers and bosses, or passing the buck for their mistakes on to employees. The result is a similar erosion of trust. Employees learn not to share their thoughts, or feel like it's pointless to put in extra effort since they'll never reap the benefits. The boss' refusal to take responsibility for their actions teaches their employees to do the same, creating a culture of blame and suspicion.

<u>Dealing with a Narcissistic Boss</u>

Narcissism is a personality disorder, and you're not going to be able to change it from the employee level. If you have other allies in leadership, you may be able to prove the narcissist's bad behavior by providing documentation of them stealing credit or passing blame. In most cases, though, the best choice is to get out of the situation as quickly as possible. If you must continue working under a narcissist boss, the best strategy is to humor them by staying on their good side and keeping your metaphorical cards close to your vest. Keep track of your work and accomplishments so you can prove you were the one who did them if the boss tries to say otherwise, and encourage trusted colleagues to do the same. As with other bad boss situations, having friends you trust among your coworkers can help you continue to make career progress and safeguard your mental health until you can get out from under the narcissist's leadership.

Overly Demanding and Critical Bosses

This type of bad boss is especially common in fast-paced workplaces with tight project deadlines, like technology, media, and entertainment. The boss' bad behavior often masquerades as necessity to cope with this high-pressure environment, and is frequently reinforced by the overall company culture. These managers lack respect for employees' boundaries and work/life balance. Even when employees deliver to their exacting standards, they may still be criticized in vague or unhelpful ways. If an employee exceeds their standards, this becomes their new standard, and the boss may expect them to achieve to this exceptional level on a consistent basis, without any recognition for the hard work they're doing.

The only redeeming quality of this type of boss is they're often just as devoted and work just as much as their team. They've internalized the concept that work is life and expect that same outlook from their employees, treating those who dare to turn down overtime or ignore evening messages as lazy low contributors. This leaves little time for team bonding or the development of a healthy culture, and burnout and turnover rates are often high under this style of leader.

Dealing with an Overly Demanding Boss
Productivity is the end-all and be-all for these managers, and to get through to them it's best to speak their language. Demonstrate why their expectations are unsustainable and how their unreasonable expectations increase waste in the form of sick days, turnover, and mistakes made

out of exhaustion, or in the quest to meet excessively tight deadlines. You're not likely to convince them that mental health is important from a human standpoint, but you can show how it impacts the bottom line and encourage them to find ways to run the team smarter rather than harder.

It's also important to set firm boundaries when you're working under this kind of boss. Make it clear when you are and are not available for communication, and if they message you outside of these times make a point of not responding. There is the risk you'll be reprimanded or disciplined, but there's also the chance you'll demonstrate that you can accomplish just as much in less time when you're given adequate time to rest. Even if the end result is termination, that's a better outcome than sacrificing your mental health for your boss' unreasonable expectations.

Can You Fix a Bad Boss?

As you can see from the sections above, the answer to this question is a resounding "it depends". The type and intent of the behavior are the main factors to consider when you're deciding how to approach the situation. Talking to trusted colleagues to get their insights on the situation can help you to clarify what strategy to take. Sometimes, your best option may be to join that 57% of people who quit a bad boss, but you may have other recourses to improve your work environment for yourself and your coworkers.

Chapter 5:
PEER-TO-PEER TOXICITY

A toxic boss is exceptionally damaging to an organizational culture and your ability as an employee to work within it. While those in leadership positions have the most influence over a workplace, however, they're not the only sources of hostility, bullying, and other forms of negativity. This kind of toxicity can also come from coworkers, and it can make the workplace just as frustrating and stressful for those who share their environment.

In some ways, navigating a toxic coworker is easier than when you have a toxic boss. They're less likely to have direct control over your career progress, for one thing, and you're not beholden to their whims the same way as if the individual is your direct supervisor. They can be equally difficult to get away from, though, and you may need to interact with them more on a day-to-day basis than you would with a toxic supervisor, which can compound the impact these engagements have on your mental health and job satisfaction.

How does toxicity manifest at the peer-to-peer level—and what can you do about it if a close team member or collaborator is making your life miserable? In this chapter, we'll take a closer look at some of the most common types of bad workplace behavior, how to spot them from your colleagues, and what to do about it if you do.

Microaggressions

For professionals from historically marginalized communities, micro-aggressions are one of the most pervasive negative behaviors encountered in the workplace. They're also one of the most difficult to address and resolve. When a coworker is passive-aggressive, lazy, or exhibits some of the other bad behaviors we'll talk about later, odds are they act this way around all of their colleagues and you can all commiserate and agree that they're difficult to work with. Micro-aggressions, however, are targeted toward specific communities. Making matters worse, those who don't belong to that community often don't notice the behavior as harmful, and frequently take the aggressor's side if the issue is brought up, assuming the victim is being too sensitive or taking things the wrong way. Because of this, many professionals of color, working women, and those from the LGBT+ community feel like they have to suffer in silence, especially when they're one of the few (or the only) from that community in their workplace.

Those who have experienced microaggressions likely need no definition. A concise description of them would be comments or actions based on stereotypes or assumptions that insult, belittle, demean, or otherwise disrespect the target. Examples could be someone hiding their purse in a drawer when a black coworker is around, when they'd normally leave it on their desk around white colleagues, or asking a transgender coworker about their genitalia, something that would never be considered appropriate workplace conversation for a cis-gender individual. They may even take the guise of a compliment, such as a female leader being praised for her assertiveness, implying surprise that she's able to take charge. These kinds of slights might seem small individually but cumulatively are very harmful to the individual's mental health and feelings of self-worth and belonging, amounting to "death by a thousand papercuts" as it's often described by those who suffer them.

Figuring out how and when to respond to microaggressions can be trying. Since they occur in the course of everyday interactions, they often go by so quickly you may not have time to realize what's happened until the conversation has already moved on. Some feel as though it's not worth quibbling over these minor moments of bias when there are other, more blatant forms of discrimination taking place elsewhere. There's also the worry of how speaking up will damage workplace relationships, not just with the perpetrator of the microaggression but also with others in their group. It's already difficult to find belonging as the office's only queer individual or one of just a few non-white team members, and many are hesitant to do anything that could make this even harder. The sheer number of microaggressions many face is another factor; many simply don't have the time or energy to respond to every single slight, and so instead they ignore all of them.

The problem is, as we mentioned, these seemingly small acts can have a big impact, both on your comfort in the office and the overall workplace. Normalizing microaggressions reinforces other biases or stereotypes that have infected the culture. They also negatively impact your ability to trust and relate to your colleagues and can trigger symptoms of past trauma, impairing your ability to work to your full capability. Even if you think you've developed a thick skin, you can still be unconsciously affected, and more so the more often you face them as you go about your work.

The first step to dealing with microaggressions is to acknowledge that they exist, recognize when they happen, and dissect the unspoken meaning and message being sent. This doesn't always mean you need to respond in the moment, or that you need to call out every single one that happens. By recognizing the instances and paying attention to patterns of who they come from and when, you can better be prepared to speak up when you're in a mental place to do so. If the perpetrator is someone you only engage with occasionally, you may decide it's not worth your effort to respond. For those you interact with on a regular basis, though, responding to their microaggressions can be empowering, and can be a big help in creating a work environment that's more inclusive for members of your community.

When you're not sure whether to respond to a chronic offender, it can be helpful to ask yourself a few questions first, such as:

- **Will my physical safety be threatened by responding?** Someone who is often violent or aggressive could fly off the handle when confronted. This doesn't mean you can never express your feelings to them, but the time and place will need to be chosen with more care. It may be better in this case to phrase your statement as a request for clarification, something like "Could you explain what you meant by that?" or "What's your thought process behind that statement?" This non-confrontational approach will be less likely to elicit emotions than a direct challenge.

- **Is this person prone to responding defensively to criticism?** Again, this doesn't mean you can't share your thoughts, but you may need expend more emotional energy during the conversation to get your point across. A helpful strategy in this case is to separate the individual from their words or actions, using words like "I know you didn't mean any harm, but..." or "You probably don't realize this, but..." that deflect the blame away from the offender.

- **Will I regret it if I don't say something?** Those conversations we feel we should have had tend to linger after the moment passes, leading to ongoing stress. In these cases, the best option is to speak up in the moment, allowing you to resolve the issue so you can move on mentally and not let the offender continue to live rent-free in your thoughts.

- **Am I tacitly accepting or condoning the behavior by not responding?** As unfair as it is, marginalized individuals are often put in the position of being advocates for their entire community. There are times staying silent will be taken as acceptance, and confronting the microaggression is the only way the individual will know their actions are not acceptable. If you're not part of the community being insulted or demeaned, using yourself as an example can be a great tactic here, saying something like "I used to think/do/say that too, but then I learned…"

- **What are my goals for this conversation?** Is your aim simply to have your voice heard? Do you hope to educate the individual about the underlying issues with what they said or did, or do you want them to change their behavior? Ideally, the former will lead to the latter, but this depends on the individual's level of self-awareness. Knowing your aims going in will help you achieve the outcome you're looking for.

Once you've answered these questions for yourself, you'll be able to create a strategy for saying what you want to say. Doing this in advance lets you seize the moment the next time a microaggression happens, rather than freezing up and saying nothing because you don't know how.

Regardless of how you deal with the offenders, finding support in your workplace can be a great help in thriving despite a coworker's microaggression. This could be other members of your community or allies within your workplace, or a support network online or among your friends who can provide an open ear for your frustrations. Self-care is also crucial. Those who are working actively toward making positive change in their community are often less affected long-term by experiencing microaggressions because it gives them some of their agency back. You may not be able to change that bigoted coworker's mind, but this at least makes you feel empowered that you're contributing in some way toward creating a more inclusive world.

Blame Culture, Backstabbing, and Credit-Stealing

A culture of blame often starts from those at the top failing to take accountability for their actions, but those within that culture tend to adopt bad behaviors even apart from the ones enacted by the leader, and these can have a ripple effect. A study by Stanford Graduate School of Business proved what those within blame cultures already knew: blame is contagious. Those who see others passing the buck for mistakes are more likely to do so themselves, regardless of where they're positioned in the hierarchy.

A blame culture arises when people feel the need to protect their ego. In some cases, this is an inborn personality trait, such as when you're dealing with a narcissist, but in many cases the cause is environmental. This same impulse leads to a variety of other negative workplace behaviors, such as:

- **Stealing credit for others' work.** This could be a coworker who claims full responsibility for a successful project when they only contributed a small amount, someone who jumps in on the credit for an effort they had no part in, or someone who overtly steals a colleague's project or effort.

- **Backstabbing.** This isn't always someone talking bad about you to superiors or coworkers. It could also be someone who sets colleagues up for failures so they can swoop in and save the day, or someone who offers help but with an unstated price or debt that they'll call in later.
- **Self-victimization.** This is the coworker who always seems to have bad things happen to them. They claim the boss or other colleagues are out to get them, or blame their failure to meet deadlines on other departments or issues from the clients. Whatever happens in their world, it seems to happen to them, as though they have no control or agency over their own actions.
- **Brown-nosing.** When praise and recognition are scarce and blame is frequent, some will respond by doing everything they can to get the boss' approval. This can include throwing colleagues under the bus if they think it will gain them status in the eyes of their supervisor.

These behaviors can arise independently, too, but if one or more of them seem to happen often in your workplace, that's a sign the environment lacks a sense of accountability. The good news is, accountability can be as contagious as blame. The best way to change this kind of culture from the employee level is to live the change you want to see. If it feels too risky to do this on your own, form an "accountability coalition" with like-minded coworkers. Agree that you will own up to mistakes that you make and publicly recognize each other for your achievements. This will have the most impact if you're in a position of seniority or leadership, but even individual contributors can help to shift this kind of culture if they commit to it.

Of course, there are times in any workplace where someone really does make a mistake and needs to be called out for it. Think carefully before you do this in a public setting, though. Often, it's more productive to have a private conversation first, where you can explain to the person what error they made and what they can learn from that moving forward. If this does need to be shared with the broader team, keep the spirit one of learning and growth, and avoid public shaming for the sheer sake of humiliation. When the failure was a team effort, keep the conversation centered on that broader picture. Don't let the conversation devolve into arguments over who made which mistake—focus on the mistakes themselves, what led to them, and how you can avoid them next time. This kind of reframing helps to remove the desire to spread blame as individuals realize they won't be penalized, ostracized, or shamed for honest errors.

Gossip and Drama

Drama queens and gossip mongers—that's so high school, right? We'd like to think that this kind of immature behavior stops once we reach adulthood and enter the workforce. Unfortunately, the people who spread rumors or made scenes in the high school halls often don't age out of these behaviors, and some of them may end up sharing your workplace. There will always be a bit of interpersonal conflict and talk about other people in any social group, but it becomes a problem when it interferes with other aspects of the culture, impeding individuals' sense of belonging or psychological safety. When the same person or set of people are always at the heart of it, this can lead to fractures in the workplace social structure, forming cliques that make some people feel excluded or attacked.

Gossip and drama are two sides of the same coin. The main difference is the focus of the unasked-for rants. With gossip, the individual responsible is spreading rumors and sensationalizing potentially harmful information about someone else in the workplace. Even if the things they're saying are true, it's often sensitive or unflattering, and not the kind of thing they'd want to have broadly spread through their peer group. With drama, the person ranting is usually at the center of the spotlight. Their rants often will involve other people, but in the context of how it affected their life. Their clients are always the most annoying, their workload the most arduous, and their interactions with the boss or coworkers the most unfair. In both cases, the person at the source of the gossip or drama thrives on chaos and creating unnecessary tension and divisions within the workplace social dynamic.

The impact of gossip and drama on your workplace can range from being a mild annoyance and time waster to causing lasting, real harm to individual's reputations, potentially damaging their careers and workplace relationships. Even when the damage is minimal, being bombarded with unwanted, potentially untrue stories about other people is draining, and doesn't create a work environment where you can be your best. In the back of your mind, you're always wondering whether those people are spreading similar rumors about you, or whether you'll misstep in the future and get caught up in their next dramatic saga.

The best first step for dealing with both drama and gossip is to not give it your attention and energy. If you don't mind a bit of confrontation, you can tell them that what they're saying about a coworker isn't nice, or push back and ask where they heard it and how they know it's true. For drama, you can provide a dose of honesty and reality, pointing out some solutions or ways they can take agency over their own choices and situation. If you'd rather not engage, you can simply tell them you're too busy with work to listen to whatever they're trying to rant about. Do this a few times and they'll often move on a choose a different target.

If you end up the target of negative gossip, the best choice is to approach it head-on. Talk to the rumor spreader and ask them why they're saying these untrue and hurtful things about you. This type of person usually dislikes direct confrontation, so if you force them into one they'll likely avoid making you a target of their rumors in the future. If it persists, it's absolutely appropriate to take them to HR or your supervisor, and you can start with this step if you don't feel comfortable approaching the gossip or drama spreader yourself.

Other Types of Bad Coworker Behavior

The negative behaviors outlined above are the most common types found in the workplace, but they're not the only ways peers can end up being toxic. Let's take a look at some other types of bad workplace behavior and what you can do about them:

Micromanagement

Someone doesn't need to have an actual management title to exhibit micromanaging behavior. At the peer level, it's most likely to come from an established senior employee who thinks they know the absolute best way to do everything and feels the need to meddle and enforce that opinion on others. Often, this behavior is well-meaning, but that doesn't make it any less annoying to have them looking over your shoulder, constantly correcting what you're doing.

The best first step for dealing with this kind of coworker is to have a calm, kind conversation about it. Tell them you appreciate their offer to help but you prefer to work independently and have your own effective way of doing things. You could even demonstrate your approach so they can see that you really do know what you're doing (and, as a bonus, getting a small taste of their own medicine could make them back off).

Passive-Aggression

These coworkers are the masters of the guilt trip. When they have an issue with something a colleague says or does, they'll never speak to them about it directly. Instead, they'll make snide comments, give them the cold shoulder, or exhibit other rude behavior as punishment for the perceived slight. This may lead to them trying to undermine your work overtly, or talking about their issues with you with others in the workplace behind your back.

Those who exhibit passive-aggressive behavior are strongly averse to conflict. Because of that, it's rarely productive to have a conversation with them about their behavior; odds are they'll deny or deflect when confronted, and you'll only deepen their bitterness in the future. Fortunately, this conflict aversion means they're relatively easy to ignore and avoid. The best solution is usually to just limit your interactions with them as much as possible to minimize the impact of their snarky comments and guilt trips on your daily work environment.

Chronic Complainers

Some people seem like they'll never be happy. When you share good news, they look for the potential ways it could go wrong—and if something bad does happen, they always assume the worst. Talking

to them, you'd think the company was always on the cusp of bank-
ruptcy, everyone's about to get fired, and every project is doomed to
failure. Sometimes, they seem to revel in bad things when they happen,
eager to share news of others people's mistakes, failures, and problems.

Everybody has bad days and needs to vent from time to time, but
dealing with someone who is constantly negative can quickly suck the
energy and life out of a workplace. The first step of dealing with these
coworkers is to tell them how their negativity is affecting you. Often,
this kind of behavior stems from their own insecurities or stress, and
they may not realize they're being such a downer. If that doesn't work,
the best option is to come up with some quick ways to gracefully escape their rants once they get going. A white lie like telling them you
have a meeting to prepare for or a phone call you need to make can
often do the trick without hurting their feelings or damaging your
work relationship.

Ostracism

Dealing with being ostracized in the workplace can be difficult because the sources of it are ambiguous. It's hard to tell if you're being
unfairly excluded, if it's a simple oversight, or if you've accidentally
offended someone with something you did or said. In many cases, ostracism arises out of bias. This may not be with the intent to harm;
when you're the only one from your background in a group, the
others may not think you want to be included, or may feel uncomfortable because they don't think you'll have common ground or are
afraid of causing offense.

The best first step when you're being ostracized is to make a conscious, active effort to be included. Tell your coworkers you'd like to
be invited the next time they have a lunch date or go out for after

work drinks. If you're lucky, they'll be happy you want to tag along. You can follow that same spirit if you notice others in your workplace are being excluded. Actively make the effort to invite them to your next gathering. If they don't take you up on it the first time, follow up and ask again so they know you're sincere and serious, and make a conscious effort to talk to them when you're around each other. Someone who's introverted may prefer to spend their time alone, but they may also just need some extra time to come out of their shell, and they will likely appreciate you at least making an effort.

If the ostracization is still happening after making this effort, the next step is to talk to the coworker you feel is the main actor of your exclusion. Ask them why they aren't including you in their activities and explain how that exclusion is making you feel. Give them the benefit of the doubt at first. Their actions may be malicious, or it may be based in an understanding; either way, you won't know until you clear the air and speak openly and honestly about the situation.

In some cases, ostracization is intentionally malicious. This is most likely to happen in a workplace with social cliques, where a "mean girls"-style dominant group aims to control who is and isn't welcome. When this is happening, there isn't much you can do about it, unfortunately. Going to your supervisor or HR could earn them a reprimand, but that's unlikely to get you included. Unfortunately, in this situation, your healthiest option may be to find a different workplace or department that's more inclusive.

Entitlement

Entitlement can have a variety of sources. In some cases, it's a personality trait of the individual, who believes they're more deserving of special treatment or allowances than others. Other times, it arises from poor management. Someone who's been habitually overlooked or under-recognized may respond by proactively demanding certain accommodations, which comes across as entitlement to those who are only seeing the responding behavior.

When you think a coworker is acting entitled, it's also important to check your own biases. Ask yourself if their demands are actually unfair related to what others receive. Someone who has a chronic illness or disability that gets to work from home when others don't isn't acting entitled, for example—they're requesting an accommodation that puts them on equal footing with their coworkers.

This is why the best approach to dealing with an entitled coworker is to find out what's motivating their behavior. Hear their side of the story before you decide that the situation is unfair, and identify exactly where their feelings are coming from. After this conversation, if you feel their demands are still unreasonable, the best solution is to set firm boundaries with that coworker that prevent them from taking advantage of you. If your coworker expects you to always stay late so that they can leave early, for example, establish a system where you trade off days and keep track of how often they put you in that situation. By documenting their instances of entitlement, you'll be better able to take them to your supervisor or HR if the situation continues—or at least to show them proof of why you feel their treatment of you is unfair.

Laziness

Working with a lazy colleague is incredibly frustrating. When there's someone in the team who's not pulling their weight, the other members have the choice of picking up their slack or allowing projects to fail. Other times, you feel the need to double-check the colleagues work for errors, or constantly check in with them to make sure work is getting done, adding unnecessary extra tasks to your plate. Just as frustrating are coworkers who are lazy about their communication, leading to work getting duplicated because they didn't tell you what they were working on, or your work not being completed on time because they never told you it needed to be done.

As with other negative coworkers, step one is going to the colleague with your issues. Be specific about the behavior that bothers you and what you would prefer that they do instead. Try not to show your frustration during this conversation. It's possible they're dropping the ball because they're struggling with depression, anxiety, or issues outside the workplace, and yelling at them isn't going to help.

While it's smart to be empathetic about your colleague's situation, you also don't want to end up in a situation where they're taking advantage of you. If they don't correct their behavior in a reasonable time frame after you tell them your issues, it's time to bring the supervisor in on the conversation. The right solution may not be a reprimand or discipline. It could be that the coworker needs to have their workload reduced, or that other accommodations can be made for extenuating circumstances. Either way, it's not your job to manage your peers—that's why teams have supervisors, and if a first conversation doesn't yield results, that's exactly when the manager needs to intervene.

Steps for Effective Conflict Resolution

Different types of negative coworkers can require slightly different approaches to improve their behavior and the overall workplace environment. While there are differences, though, there are also commonalities. In all these cases, effective communication is key to identifying and resolving the issue. Conflicts will inevitably arise within any group of people, and the more diverse their personalities and background, the higher the odds of conflict become. While it's uncomfortable, the conflict itself isn't the issue. There are some types of conflict that are overtly harmful, like bullying or harassment (which we'll go into in more depth in a later chapter). In many instances, though, these disputes can end up being productive, leading to improvements and positive change for the culture or workplace procedures. Problems arise when that conflict is allowed to continue unchecked and infect the broader culture.

With that in mind, the general best steps for resolving any conflict in the workplace are:

1. **Identify the source of the conflict.** This means talking to both sides, even if one seems to be the clear aggressor and the other the clear victim. People are more open to considering other points of view when they feel they're being heard, so listening to both sides is an important first step.

2. **Collaborate to analyze and discuss the situation.** Weigh and consider all the perspectives. If anger, frustration, and other negative emotions arise, take a pause to recalibrate and regain calm. Make sure the conversation doesn't devolve into personal attacks or accusations that can steer it in an unproductive direction.

3. **Work together to reach a solution that works for everyone.** Use the information shared during the conversation to find points of commonality and identify exactly what each side sees as the problem, and what they want to have done about it. It may take some time to come to complete agreement, but don't give up—even if it's hard, there is always a solution.

4. **Implement the solution and follow-up to ensure the conflict-ing behavior changes.** It's often not enough to just tell people what you want them to do. It takes time to unlearn old habits and replace them with new, healthier behaviors. Be firm in expecting everyone to follow the new behavior standards, and establish consequences of failing to do so that you can employ if they become necessary.

These steps don't necessarily need to be enacted by a manager. Conflict resolution within a team is sometimes the better option, and a neutral colleague who's trusted by both parties can be a very effective mediator.

Whatever type of conflict and negativity you're dealing with in your workplace, it's important to remember that you can't change other people's behavior. You can only control how you respond to it, and communicate with them to encourage them to change themselves. Allowing all parties to maintain their full agency is the only way to achieve meaningful, lasting improvements.

Chapter 6:
WHEN BAD APPLES SPOIL THE BUNCH

In chapter 4, we discussed the ways in which a toxic manager can corrupt the culture of an organization. Leaders also have the power to be a force for good, though, and not every negative work environment starts from the top. Individual contributors can also make a workplace downright unbearable for their colleagues if no one steps in to correct their behavior (or remove them from the team, when they resist these attempts at change).

Just because leaders have the ability to improve a work environment doesn't always mean they have the knowledge and tools to do so. This type of culture correction is rarely covered in management training courses, leaving well-meaning leaders to their own devices when it comes to fixing problems with their organization's culture. Even identifying the source of the toxicity can be difficult, especially if the ones spreading it act differently when the boss is around. Not every conflict between employees is a sign of toxicity, either. Sometimes, people simply disagree or have a clash of personality, calling for a more two-sided approach to conflict resolution than when a single employee is causing problems for other members of the team.

So how can you identify when you have a bad apple in your team—and what should you do about it if you do? Let's break down some steps to answer each of those questions.

Identifying Toxic Team Members

Some bad employee behaviors are obvious—if you hear someone make a blatantly racist remark, for example, or witness one employee sexually harassing another. Often, though, bad employee behavior is either more subtle or happens out of your direct view. In these instances, you as the manager need to do some investigative work and piece together the signs to differentiate between employee disagreements, issues stemming from the over-arching culture, and problems that are the direct result of a report.

The good news is, there are some signs that, while not always present when you have a toxic employee, are frequent indicators that a single individual contributor is bringing down your team's morale. You can pair these with the types of toxic coworkers described in the previous chapter, too, which can help identify the specific flavor of bad apple that you're dealing with.

<u>Sign #1: Nobody wants to work with them.</u>

This one might seem obvious, but very often it goes ignored by managers when in the process of investigating the cause of a morale drop or spike in absenteeism and turnover. Most people want to avoid conflict, and that includes talking poorly about someone to the person in charge. Rather than report their problems with the bad apple to you directly, they may instead aim to distance themselves from the individual who is causing them stress, citing vague reasons that avoid pinning the blame on their coworker.

If this only happens sporadically, that likely points to more of a simple personality clash, and is not something you necessarily need to investigate further. The red flag raises when most or all of the others on the team seem to have an issue working with the same person. Note that this only shows you who the problem employee might be; more research will be needed to identify the reason the rest of the team seems to shun them. It could be an issue with their competence and knowledge rather than their behavior—people are just as likely to avoid working with someone who needs constant supervision or correction of their work as they are to avoid someone who's hostile or overly negative. Do this research quietly and cautiously; you don't want to inadvertently cause new drama in your drive to correct an existing problem.

<u>Sign #2: Overconfidence.</u>

This one can be tricky because confidence is by and large seen as a positive trait in most workplaces. Being self-assured and knowledgeable is a good thing. When that goes too far, though, it turns into cockiness and arrogance. People with these traits tend to have difficulty taking accountability for their mistakes, and may have a self-centered view of the workplace, focusing only on the way things affect them rather than considering their colleagues or the company as a whole. Overconfidence is also a sign of other issues that can make someone a problem for the organization, like narcissism, and may be one of the few signs of them, since individuals with this trait are often adept at blame deflection and manipulation, allowing them to hide their worse traits from superiors at the same time they make colleagues' lives miserable.

<u>Sign #3: They're a frequent source of gossip and drama.</u>

Sometimes, good employees can get inadvertently caught up in the rumor mill, or find themselves in the middle of the latest office drama. More often than not, though, your bad apples will be the ones spreading the rumors and causing the drama. This is another sign you need to be cautious in exploring further—you don't want your employees to see you going around asking for the latest tea and take that as a sign gossip is okay. It is also the nature of gossip that it spreads beyond its original source, so the employee you hear saying it could well not have been the one who started it. A private chat with anyone involved in drama or spreading rumors, especially harmful ones, can be a useful way to hone in on the original source.

<u>Sign #4: They shoot down others' ideas but rarely contribute their own.</u> Constructive criticism can be a helpful thing during collaboration sessions, helping the team to identify and plan for problems and refine their ideas to arrive at the best possible solution. The key here is that the critique is productive, focusing on specific problems and presenting potential solutions or workarounds. Employees who only seem to focus on negative "what if?"s during meetings likely bring that same negativity to other areas of their workday, and could be sapping the energy from the rest of your team in the process.

<u>Sign #5: The make offensive jokes or stereotyped comments.</u>
An ethnic joke may not be intended to cause harm, and depending on your environment and the people in it, it may not be directly offensive to the people who hear it. Even so, it is a bad sign that the individual is holding biases, either consciously or unconsciously, and that can lead to other, forms of discrimination. The fact that they make an off-color comment out loud also indicates they think this is acceptable behavior in your organization, so this is both a sign of a potentially toxic employee and an indication you have some issues to address at the systemic level. The same goes if you witness or hear a microaggression.

Even if no one on the team calls it out, that doesn't mean it should be allowed to continue, and you should keep an eye on that employee to see if they're making colleagues uncomfortable in other ways.

<u>Sign #6: You catch them in a lie.</u>
Everybody makes mistakes, and sometimes that could take the form of saying something untrue. It could be something they were told and believed, for example, or they could remember a situation incorrectly. Outright lies are a more troublesome matter, though. Someone who will willfully, knowingly lie is more likely to be dishonest in other ways, like cheating or stealing, making it impossible for you to trust them as an employee. It also means they likely exhibit this same behavior with their coworkers, sapping trust out of those relationships and making it impossible to maintain a transparent, healthy, and collaborative workplace.

Identifying outright lies from honest mistakes can be difficult. Someone who knowingly lied could well claim it was an error when they are called out on it, and proving intent can be a challenge. That said, catching an employee in a lie is a sign you should quietly keep your eye on them to ensure it truly was an error rather than a habit.

<u>Sign #7: They act like they're the manager.</u>
Senior employees who take newer team members under their wing are a positive force, providing informal mentorship that can help newer hires integrate into the workplace. There is a fine line, however, between someone who guides their colleagues and someone who meddles in other people's work. Not only can this damage their colleagues' confidence and rob them of their agency, it also diminishes your authority as the manager, impairing your ability to positively impact the

workplace. If an employee seems to always be hovering over someone else's desk or correcting their work without being asked, pay close attention to see if the employee on the receiving end views it as helpful assistance or an unwelcome intrusion.

What To Do About a Toxic Employee?

On first blush, the answer to this might seem obvious: get rid of them. While this may ultimately prove to be your solution, though, it isn't always that easy. Workplace toxicity can be difficult to prove, potentially opening the door for damaging or costly litigation. In other cases, the employee may have skills or knowledge that are hard to replace, or may have value in other areas that you (or your superiors) would prefer not to lose.

Whatever the reason, managers often need to find another way to remove or mitigate the damage caused by a toxic employee, or at least be able to demonstrate a good faith attempt at having done so. For those in this situation, here are some steps to follow.

Step 1: Analyze the behavior and identify its cause.

In many instances, toxicity is a symptom of a deeper problem. The individual could feel frustrated with their own career progress and be lashing out at colleagues as a result. Other times, people are rude or say hurtful things because of internal or personal struggles, such as mental health issues like depression, anxiety, addiction, or stressors and tragedies at home.

Before you take any drastic steps, have a one-on-one with the employee and ask how they're doing, both at work and at home. They may immediately reveal a background struggle or issue that explains their behavior. Note that we said explain, not excuse; their behavior is still unacceptable, but your method for dealing with it can be gentler. It may be appropriate to help them connect with counseling services, or to suggest they take a vacation or sabbatical.

If no outside sources for their toxicity readily present themselves, explain the specific behavior that's a problem and how it impacts the team. Some people may not realize they come across as aggressive or may be unaware of their biases, and a nudge from a supervisor can help them correct their behavior on their own. While you should be specific about the behavior and give concrete examples, be careful not to reveal any individual coworkers who have made complaints against the individual during this conversation. Vague statements like "I've noticed you…" or "It has come to my attention that…" can shield colleagues' identities so their interactions with the toxic team member aren't affected moving forward.

Whichever way the conversation plays out, document it fully, just in case things don't improve and you need a paper trail to justify future consequences. End by working with them to set improvement goals, giving them specific behaviors you'd like to see instead and a timeline within which you expect their behavior to change.

Step 2: Observe and reinforce.

Anyone who has tried to quit smoking or drinking caffeine knows that habits are hard to break. Even if the employee is genuinely trying to improve, it may take some time for the old, toxic behaviors to be replaced by healthier ones. Watch the problem employee's interactions and behavior between your first conversation and your follow-up meeting. Document any continuing issues you notice, as well as notable changes or corrections you see them making, so you can discuss their efforts fully during their next conversation.

While you want to keep an eye on the employee, you don't want them to feel like you're looking over their shoulder all the time. Part of observing should be talking to previous victims of their toxicity about how the employee acts when outside your direct supervision, or other indirect forms of observation. If you directly see the individual falling into old bad habits, gently but firmly remind them of the new expectations, and document that you gave this reminder.

Step 3: Assign consequences.
Ideally, the employee will have made genuine steps toward improving by the time you have your follow-up meeting. The behavior may not be completely eradicated, but if there has been a noticeable positive shift, you can give positive reinforcement for the changes thus far and continue working with them to further the improvement.

If not, it's time to take a harder approach. Some people respond better when there are potential negative consequences for their actions, and the time has come to outline what those will be. This starts by identifying the individual's pain point. Identify what it will hurt them the most to lose, whether that's an upcoming monetary bonus, a chance at a promotion, the right to work remotely, or some other workplace perk. Again, set a clear timeline for improvement, at which point they will receive the consequence if there has been no observable change in their behavior—and, as before, thoroughly document the conversation, including having them sign an acknowledgment that they are aware of their expectations and the consequences of not achieving them.

Step 4: Removal or isolation.
Unfortunately, some people cannot or will not change their behavior. By this point, you should have enough documentation of their repeated

bad behavior and your attempts to correct it that you can terminate them should you choose to do so.

If there are outside circumstances that take the option of termination off the table, it's time to isolate them as much as you can from the rest of the team. This could be imposing more physical distance by relocating their desk or giving them more work that can be done from home, or psychological distance in the form of removing them from collaborative projects in lieu of more independent work. You should also be mindful of other forms of toxicity that arise around the situation, like colleagues gossiping about the toxic employee, and make it clear that this behavior isn't acceptable, either.

At the same time, providing additional support to the rest of the team can help isolate them mentally and emotionally from the impact of the toxic team member's actions and attitude. Managing a toxic employee can eat up a lot of your time and energy as a manager, and you want to make sure you're not neglecting the rest of your team in the process. Providing positive energy to replace the negativity introduced by the toxic employee can also help restore the broader culture. Be generous with your praise when they deliver strong work, and make a point of celebrating both individual and team accomplishments. Make a point of re-building the confidence of team members who were belittled or dismissed by their toxic colleague through positive reinforcement and acknowledgment of their skills and effort. With diligence, you can undo the damage caused by the problem employee and prevent them from having further detrimental effects on the team, even if you're unable to remove them entirely.

Preventing Toxicity Through Policy

Toxic employees can exist in any kind of workplace, but they are more likely to thrive in one that has unhealthy workplace norms. Replacing these norms with healthier policies and processes can both help the team recover from the effects of a bad colleague and prevent future problem employees from having as profound of an effect. Some of the best policies for eliminating and preventing toxicity include:

- **Robust employee feedback systems.** Listening to your staff's concerns is step number one for eliminating toxicity. A well-designed feedback system can clue you into problems you don't see before they can cause lasting damage.
- **Set reasonable deadlines and work hours.** An overworked, stressed employee is more likely to lash out than one who is well-rested, happy, and has a good work/life balance. Reducing overtime, giving ample notice for major projects, and providing adequate PTO (that employees are actually able to use) can all help to maintain a healthy workplace.
- **Increase employee flexibility.** Hybrid schedules and employee agency over schedules can also give a major boost to work/life balance, and are another tool in your arsenal for reducing drama and stress in your team.
- **More transparency.** Share information about your decision-making process, major projects, upcoming changes in the business, or anything else that affects the employees' day-to-day. This will help prevent speculation and work-related gossip. Along these same lines, giving employees more of a voice in decisions restores their agency and makes it less likely toxicity will develop.

- **Peer-to-peer rewards.** It feels good to be acknowledged, and the boss doesn't have to be the only one with this power. Allowing employees to reward each other when they see strong work and good behavior makes them more likely to make good choices in their daily interactions.

The Best Solution

Combining a top-down and bottom-up approach can be effective in reducing the impacts of a toxic report. Even so, rooting out a toxic employee can be difficult and time-consuming. Maybe the best way to save yourself that trouble is to not hire them in the first place—easier said than done, certainly, but there are ways you can spot a potential problem employee during the hiring process.

First, pay attention to how they act on their interview day. Did they arrive at the correct time, or did they disrespect your time by showing up late? When interacting with assistants, parking attendants, and other employees, were they civil and respectful, or did they act like these individuals were below them? If the candidate is polite with the leader but rude to lower members of the hierarchy, this is a major red flag of toxicity.

Following up with the candidate's references and members of your professional network can provide insights, as well. When talking to the reference, pay attention to their non-verbal cues, like their tone and pacing of answers. Make sure you ask the right questions, too. If they were in a managerial role, find out how their subordinates responded under their leadership. When speaking to your network, focus on their experience working with the individual and whether they would want to work with them again.

There are also questions you can ask during the interview to weed out toxic candidates. Some great ones include:

- What kind of people do you find difficult to work with?
- How would your former coworkers describe you?
- What is one trait about yourself that you would like to improve?
- What is a time that you failed in the workplace? What did you learn from that experience, and what could you have done in hindsight to prevent it?

Again, pay attention not just to what they answer, but how. Does their answer seem genuine or rehearsed? When asked about mistakes, do they own up to their role or shift the blame? You may not catch every bad apple before they make it onto your team, but focusing on attitude and behavior during the interview process—not just competence—can be a big step in the right direction.

Chapter 7:
COPING WITH HARRASSMENT, BULLYING AND ABUSE

In a 2017 survey by the Workplace Bullying and Trauma Institute, they found that 19% of workers have been personally bullied or harassed while on the job, and a similar percentage of respondents had seen this kind of behavior happen to someone else. This means some 60 million American workers are affected by bullying in any given year. Of those respondents who had been bullied, 40% experienced health problems related to the stress and trauma. More disturbing, nearly a third (29%) of those who were targets of bullying reported they stayed silent about the abuse. This is likely a direct result of the WBTI's findings that 71% of employer reactions to reported harassment or bullying ended up being harmful to the target of the bullying.

Harassment, bullying, and abuse are the most harmful forms of workplace toxicity, both from the perspective of the victim and for the organizations where they happen—and, as these findings show, they are a significant problem that affects a wide range of industries and workplaces.

What Exactly Are Bullying and Harassment?

The terms abuse, bullying, and harassment are near-synonyms but there are key differences between them, and understanding these differences can help you to clarify your experiences as a victim. Abuse can be broadly defined as repeatedly treating another person cruelly or violently. Bullying is a specific type of abuse, in which one individual or a group of individuals repeatedly use cruelty to intimidate and harm someone weaker or less powerful. Note that bullying doesn't have to be against someone who is objectively in a position of weakness. A strong-willed report could still bully a manager whom they see as weak and lacking in authority; the weakness, in this case, is in the eye of the abuser.

Within a workplace context, harassment is the most specific of these terms. It describes mistreatment of an individual due to their identity as a member of a protected class. This could include their gender, sexual orientation or gender identity, race, ethnicity, religion, age, or disability status.

The main reason this distinction matters is because harassment is illegal in the United States (and many other countries), while bullying is not. Your organization may have rules of its own against broader forms of bullying and abuse, but it is only prosecutable under the law if the mistreatment is due to the victim's belonging to a protected class. The exception to this is if the bullying escalates into behaviors that are sufficient basis for prosecution or a civil suit, such as assault, stalking, or defamation.

Identifying Workplace Abusers

The WBTI's 2017 survey found that the majority of workplace bullies (61%) are bosses. This makes a certain kind of sense. Bullying, as we mentioned above, is defined by someone mis-treating an individual they see as weaker, and those in a position of authority are the ones who have the power in workplace relationships. Added to this is the fact that people are more reluctant to stand up for themselves against someone higher up in the hierarchy, allowing negative behavior to escalate to the point of bullying.

While bosses are the most frequent abusers, however, harassment can come from anywhere in an organization, including peer-to-peer abuse and bullying by a report against a manager. Regardless of its source, it can be difficult for the targets of bullying to definitively identify their treatment as abuse, especially in its early stages, when the abuser may not be yet at their worst behavior. Self-doubt and gaslighting can impair the victim's judgment of the behavior's severity, or they may rationalize the behavior out of a desire to see the best in people, or from fear of being seen as over-sensitive if they do broach the subject with the aggressor and others in the organization.

So how can you decide if what you're experiencing is bullying, harassment, or abuse, as opposed to another type of workplace conflict? There are three core defining traits to look for:

1. **It is targeted.** Bullies and abusers have specific individuals who are the focus of their misbehavior. With others, their behavior could range from sullen and combative to downright charming, but they are only outright cruel or violent with specific individuals.

2. **It is repeated or habitual.** A single screaming outburst from a boss does not automatically earn them the label of "bully." Rather, bullying and abuse are patterns of ongoing behavior, often increasing in severity or frequency over time.

3. **It is done with intent.** A bully or abuser sets out to hurt, tear down, or weaken their target, often with the aim of asserting their own dominance and power. Microaggressions and other unintentionally degrading or offensive comments might still cause lasting harm to the target, but those alone aren't enough to make the offender a bully since they are not intended to do harm.

The harm caused by bullying can be either physical or psychological (or, in some cases, both). While bullies are often aggressive, this is not always the case, either. There are a range of hurtful behaviors that can be included under the broader umbrellas of bullying or harassment. Some of the most common include:

Discriminatory Harassment

This is the type of harassment that is illegal, and is defined as harassment directed at an employee because of their race, age, gender, religious beliefs, or disability. The exact behaviors could include any of those described below, but their motivation and content is specifically related to the trait that puts the victim in a protected class. The main reason to be attuned to this as a victim is that, since it is prohibited by law, you may have a wider range of options available

Aggressive Communication

The most visible example of this is a manager who regularly berates or screams at reports, or a coworker who makes public scenes, yelling at a colleague in front of customers or other employees. It also includes aggressive or threatening body language and gestures, and in modern hybrid or remote workplaces may be shifted into text form with angry all-caps emails or text messages. Public forms of aggressive communication are damaging to everyone who witnesses them, not only the specific target. These displays create a culture of fear, causing individuals to dread their time around that boss or colleague, unsure whether they'll become the next target of their anger. Victims are similarly afraid to defend themselves or reporting the behavior, who endure the abuse because they fear it will only make it worse if they try to stop it.

Physical Violence

Physical violence isn't only limited to slapping or grabbing another person. It could also be violence against inanimate objects, like throwing things or punching walls. Similar to screaming or shouting, physical violence intimidates the victim through fear. In some cases, such as if the bully breaks your personal property or does you physical harm, it could be considered assault. If you are the victim of this type of bullying, talk to a lawyer about your potential legal options.

Disparagement and Humiliation

These behaviors are intended to make victims doubt their own value and worth. It could take the form of constant criticism, even for minor issues or in spite of overall high performance. The bully will downplay their victim's successes and overblow their mistakes. As with aggression, this could be done privately or in front of colleagues, with the aim of publicly humiliating the victim. It may also take the form of jokes at the victim's expense, pulling embarrassing pranks, spreading harmful rumors aimed at damaging your reputation, or publicly mocking your work quality, appearance, or capability.

When called out on their behavior, this type of bully will often use gaslighting and deflection to convince their victim that they have either overreacted to or misinterpreted their statements. Often, they use humor as a shield, framing the victim as the unreasonable one who "can't take a joke". A disparaging boss may claim the abuse is critical feedback, or justify their behavior as having high expectations or being "demanding". This makes it very hard for victims of this type of bullying to verify that their feels are rational and legitimate. Remember the three qualifications of bullying: it is targeted, habitual, and has the intent to harm. As the victim, documenting your interactions with the individual, while at the same time observing their interactions with others, can help to clarify the situation.

Manipulation

One common form of manipulation in the workplace is when a bully takes a transactional approach to their relationship with the victim. They create a situation in which the victim needs them, then attach some kind of price to their aid. Examples could be a manager offering a promotion in exchange for unpaid overtime, or a coworker who refuses to share necessary information unless you cover for them leaving early. Bullies also often use manipulative behaviors like guilt trips and shunning. If the bully is in a leadership position, they may selectively "forget" to invite you to a meeting or inform you of a project deadline, then scream at you after the fact for missing it.

Bullies often wear different masks depending on who they are interacting with, and this kind of manipulation makes it very hard to stand up for yourself as a victim. They may use gossip or public shaming to tarnish your reputation in the team or with leadership, discrediting you should you attempt to call them out. This also serves to isolate you from colleagues, preventing the formation of trust bonds with other so that you rely on the bully more as a source of support.

Cyberbullying

Cyberbullying is an increasing problem in the workplace as more and more companies adopt remote or hybrid workplaces. It can also include social media interactions between team members, threatening or offensive messages sent via messaging systems or email, or any kind of bad behavior that happens online. This harassment may be directed at the victim or be more indirect, like spreading damaging rumors through social media or backstabbing and discrediting the individual in a team messenger system, or by forwarding a private message or email to leadership without the victim's consent or knowledge. If you're the victim of cyberbullying, make sure to take screenshots and save messages to establish a record of the behavior, even if the bully's actions are taken anonymously, or on a social media platform outside the workplace.

Power Harassment

This is when the bully exploits a power imbalance between them and their victim. Most often, that power disparity is based on the hierarchy, like in a manager/report situation, but it can also be a coworker exploiting their greater social power or seniority to take advantage of younger colleague. The person in power can exert their control through a variety of behaviors, like making extreme demands on their time, giving excessive or overly harsh criticism, or violating their boundaries and work/life balance by contacting them at all hours of the night and weekend, or prying into their personal life. The bully's power (or perceived power) over the victim carries the implied threat that they will lose status in the workplace, or even lose their job, if they protest against the bullying behavior.

<u>Retaliation</u>

This could be a bully targeting a victim because out of jealousy for an accomplishment or a perceived slight against them. An example might be a coworker who starts undermining and belittling you after you receive a promotion they were also in the running for. In other cases, bullies will take retaliatory action against those who report or push back against their behavior. This is not necessarily isolated to the original victim. A colleague who sees the bully attacking someone and calls them out on it publicly could then find themselves the new target of the behavior, which then serves to make other coworkers less likely to speak up against them in the future.

Sexual Harassment

Perhaps the most misunderstood form of workplace bullying is sexual harassment. It is also unfortunately pervasive, and in some industries has long been an unspoken and accepted practice, a reality that has only in the past few decades come into question. While sexual harassment is illegal, it can also be exceptionally difficult to prove, particularly in cases where the harasser is a boss or other authority figure.

One especially harmful misconception about sexual harassment is that all perpetrators are male and all victims are female. These are the most commonly reported instances of sexual harassment, but that figure likely does not tell the whole story. Those who identify as male or non-binary can also be the targets of sexual harassment, and female or non-binary individuals can be the aggressor. Unfortunately, instances of harassment that fall outside the accepted "male on female" archetype are significantly less likely to be reported, or to be treated as serious issues if they are.

Part of this problem stems from another misconception about sexual harassment: that it is about sexual attraction. That may be a factor in how the harasser chooses their victims, but like other forms of bullying, sexual harassment is really about control and power. A lesbian manager making obscene gestures or sending explicit photos to a gay male report is still sexual harassment; the likelihood that a sexual relationship would form between the abuser and victim should never be a factor in that determination.

The situation is also often complicated by the broader complexities of interpersonal workplace relationships. For those observing from the outside, it can be difficult to differentiate consensual, two-sided workplace flirting or mutual relationships like "work spouses" from sexual harassment, particularly when the aggressor and victim have differing stories about the nature of their relationship. This leads to a "he said/she said" situation for those who report it, and when the aggressor is in leadership or a more senior team member, their more established relationship with decision makers gives them an upper hand in these discussions. That power difference is compounded by any unconscious biases among leadership, such as if they don't believe female-identifying individuals can be sexual aggressors, or if the aggressor is part of a protected class and leaders hesitate to discipline them out of fear of being seen as racist, sexist, or homophobic.

The key difference between harmless workplace flirting and sexual harassment is consent. Harassment is unwelcome attention of a sexual nature. It also includes Quid Pro Quo sexual harassment, in which there is a stated or implied workplace benefit for the victim if they consent to unwanted sexual attention. In these situations, the victim may actually be the initiator because they view it as their only means of advancing their career or obtaining job security. An example would be a workplace in which the only female employees who receive raises or promotions are those who flirt with the boss. In this case, the boss may not directly solicit the flirtation, but the established culture and behavior patterns convey a message that this is the only avenue to career progress. Even if there isn't an established culture of harassment, the power dynamic between bosses and reports often complicate the situation for victims. The behavior may initially seem like welcome, friendly banter that is building a positive report between the victim and their superior. The interactions could start with seemingly innocent jokes or compliments of the employee's appearance, for example, evolving over time into invasive questions, unnecessary and excessive one-on-one meetings, texts or calls outside of work hours, or requests for unreasonable favors. By the time the victim is uncomfortable and realizes there's a problem, they often feel it's too late to speak up and set boundaries, or fear doing so will disrupt their work environment or threaten their continued employment.

Sexual harassment can include a range of actions and behaviors, such as:

- **Inappropriate physical contact.** This includes overtly sexual contact as well as more subtle touching, like lingering hugs, massages, holding an employee's arm or shoulder, or sitting/standing uncomfortably close during meetings or social outings.

- **Invasions of personal space.** Within the workplace, this could be hovering over the victim's desk while they're working, seeking out the victim during their breaks or lunch, or violating their work/life boundaries by prying for personal information or communications and requests during their free time that are unrelated to work (e.g. a flirtatious text sent at 2AM, asking the employee to run personal errands on the weekend, expectations to attend non-work related dinners, etc.)

- **Sexual comments, questions, requests, or jokes.** These may be directed at the employee, like a verbal request for a sexual favor, repeated comments on their appearance, or questions about the employee's sex life. It also includes sexualized comments about coworkers made to the victim, or the aggressor discussing their sex life or sexual fantasies.
- **Romantic gifts.** Getting a nice watch or edible bouquet from the boss in recognition of a workplace achievement isn't necessarily a sign of a problem. However, if the gifts are only given to the victim, are romantic in nature (e.g. roses on Valentine's Day), or are sexual in nature (e.g. receiving lingerie from a coworker), that is a red flag of harassment.
- **Circulating pornography or sexually suggestive photos.** These may be targeted at the victim or circulated broadly throughout the team, and could be images of the victim, the aggressor, other coworkers, or individuals unrelated to the workplace who are nude or in a suggestive pose.

Whatever the specific behaviors involved, if they're offensive, invasive, or create a hostile work environment, it qualifies as sexual harassment under the law.

Coping with Abusive Peers and Reports

The next chapter will address the reporting process should you decide to go to HR, leadership, or an outside legal team to deal with your workplace bully. This process can be both long and traumatic, however, and unfortunately doesn't always guarantee the issue will be resolved (and may have negative consequences for the victim, depending on the workplace culture).

The good news is, there are other steps you can take before reporting to safeguard your physical and psychological safety, and taking these steps will help to prove your case if and when you do report.

1. **Speak up as soon as you become a target.** Telling the bully their behavior is not okay when it first starts sends the message you aren't an easy target, and can prevent the behavior from becoming habitual. Use similar strategies to those outlined for toxic colleagues. Call out the behavior rather than the person, be specific about the problem and what they should do instead, and appeal to their or the company's values (e.g. "I know you value inclusiveness, but when you say/do [specific action] it makes me uncomfortable because [reason it's wrong]. In the future, I expect [desired outcome/behavior change].")

2. **Document both the behavior and your performance.** This is very beneficial for reporting, but it also helps you stay connected to reality and prove that you're not "crazy" or "oversensitive." Write down exactly what happened as soon as you can after you experience harassment, including the date/time, location, and if any colleagues witnessed the interaction. Save or screenshot any cyberbullying or interactions that happen through text or email. Finally, keep a record of your own performance, so you can defend against their unwarranted critiques of your work quality, or demonstrate the impact the bullying had on your ability to work if you need to report it down the line.

3. **Review the organization's bullying and harassment policies.**
    Even though personal bullying is not illegal, many organiza-
    tions have conduct standards for employees, and your bully
    is likely violating at least one. Research these rules to help you
    plan the wisest course of action moving forward if the harass-
    ment continues.

4. **Impose boundaries and distance when possible.** Some work-
    places have the option of gaining more physical distance,
    whether by moving to a new desk or taking advantage of a
    hybrid environment to limit your time around the bully. In re-
    mote workplaces, steps could include blocking private mes-
    sages from the bully or interacting with them only in threads
    and calls involving other colleagues.

5. **Focus on self-care.** Being bullied tears you down, and until
    you can make the behavior stop, it's important to do things
    that build you back up. This could mean spending time with
    friends and family, using PTO to take a vacation or devote
    time to a passion project, or speaking with a therapist.

These same steps also apply when you see bullying happening to
someone else in your workplace. They may be too scared or shy to
speak up for themselves, but as an observer your stakes are lower,
especially if you already have an established rapport or social clout
with the bully. Assess the situation to decide if it's best to have this
conversation privately or to call the behavior out in the moment.
Doing it in public can be safer for you if the bully is aggressive or violent, and can empower others who witness it to follow your lead,
but a private conversation is often less likely to trigger defensive reactions and can be more productive in some cases.

Coping with Abusive Leaders

The suggested steps above still apply when your bully is your boss, but the situation can be much more complicated. You have fewer options for reporting, for one thing, and reporting may be less effective if the bully has already tarnished your reputation with other leaders. It also may not be possible to establish boundaries or get distance when the harasser is your direct superior.

In these situations, a helpful extra step to take is to observe the boss' interactions with others, and how your coworkers respond when they witness you being bullied. This can help you to identify potential allies or other victims within the team, forming a coalition so you don't have to take on the bullying boss on your own. If you do report, this support can help ensure your issue is acknowledged.

Unfortunately, being in a position of lower authority limits your options for ending or evading negative behavior. Take a moment to weigh the advantages of staying with your organization against the negative impacts of the harassment or abuse on your mental health and work ability. Honestly consider how likely you are to succeed if you attempt to remove the boss or change their behavior. If there is a culture of turning a blind eye to managerial misbehavior, the healthiest and best option in the long-term is often to cut your losses and find a better work environment.

Leadership's Role in Workplace Bullying

Individuals are responsible for their own behavior, but the culture of the organization is what allows them to get away with it. Some bullies hide their behavior from leaders or ingratiate themselves to decision makers; others may be more obviously toxic, but are seen as too valuable to let go because of their performance or unique skills. By not responding to the behavior, however, leaders tacitly approve of it and become complicit in the abuse or harassment.

Effective anti-harassment policies are the best way to limit it in your organization. This starts with updating the workplace policies to define appropriate and inappropriate behavior and outline consequences for violating these standards. It also means having a straightforward reporting system that allows victims anonymity and safety from reprisal. Learn to recognize the common signs of harassment, bullying, and abuse, and train your staff—especially those in people management positions—on how to spot and respond to this behavior among reports. The bullying itself may be targeted but its consequences and impact can affect the entire organization, so it is worth the time and effort to put a stop to the current behavior and create systems that will prevent it in the future.

Chapter 8

REPORTING PROBLEMS (AND DEALING WITH THE AFTERMATH)

The process of reporting workplace harassment, discrimination, or bullying can sometimes feel just as frustrating and nerve-wracking as the behavior you're experiencing. Most don't know until they make the report how their company will react, and making a report only to be brushed aside—or to be disciplined yourself while your aggressor goes unpunished—can be both traumatic and damaging for your career. This is why many workplace issues go unreported, with the victim either suffering through the abuse or quitting in search of a better work environment.

Sometimes, quitting is the best option, especially when the problems in the organization are pervasive and deeply entrenched. This shouldn't be your only option, though. Employees who are victims of harassment and discrimination have the right to report the behavior, to expect their company to intervene and correct the issue, and to be free from retaliation or other mistreatment after making their report. These rights are enforced at the federal level by the U.S. Equal Employment Opportunity Commission (EEOC), who can act on your behalf directly if your company's reporting system fails to resolve the issue. While much of the reporting process is out of the employee's control, you can help yourself to get the best outcome by following the right steps in a timely manner and maintaining detailed documentation of both the behavior that prompted the report and how your company responds to it.

Preparing to Report

You don't want to delay too long when you're reporting workplace issues. For one thing, bullying and harassment often gets worse over time, so reporting the individual early can spare you the experience of that escalation. The EEOC can also only take action on incidents that happened within the last 180 days, and they'll want to see that you've gone through all your options within the company first, so starting the process early ensures you'll be fully protected. Having said that, however, there are steps you should take before you file a report that won't take long to prepare, and can greatly improve your odds of success.

Step 1: Document the behavior.

The more proof you have to back up your claim, the harder it will be for your company to brush off your concerns, or for the person you are reporting to say you are overreacting or lying. As we said in the last chapter, the best choice is to document behaviors as they occur by maintaining a written log of the behavior, when and where it happened, and who was around to witness it. Because behavior tends to escalate over time, you may not have thought to document early, less egregious behaviors when they happened. In that case, it's still smart to write a record of the behavior, including as much specificity as you can remember. This establishes a pattern of behavior, which will be important further along in the process if you need to go to an outside reporting agency.

Along with your written record of events, you should save other records that can prove the discrimination or harassment. Federal law protects employees against work-related discrimination and harassment even when you're outside the physical workplace, including harassment that happens online or at off-site functions like conferences or work social events. This is why you should keep track of all interactions and evidence, including:

- Written correspondence like emails, text messages, or social media posts
- Photos and images, both those sent to you (e.g. if a coworker sends you nude pictures) and pictures documenting their behavior (e.g. bruises from a physical altercation, damage they caused to a vehicle or other personal item, etc.)
- Physical items, both those given to you (e.g. inappropriate gifts given to you by a sexually harassing supervisor), or items they damaged (along with receipts and records if you had them repaired, cleaned, or replaced)
- A separate list of witnesses who observed the behavior, or other victims of the behavior who can reinforce your claim
- Medical records of treatment you had to get because of the harassment, including mental health treatment
- Your personnel file and paystubs, to show a record of your performance and how it was impacted by the discrimination or harassment

This process of documentation may involve talking about your situation with select colleagues. You may want to verify your memories of past events, for example, and can ask a coworker who witnessed it for their account. Similarly, discussing your experiences with other targets of the behavior can help to clarify your experiences and show that they aren't isolated incidents. However, you should avoid general complaints and discussion of your experiences with coworkers who are not involved. This can lead to gossip that will only muddle the picture during future investigations, especially since details tend to warp and change as facts pass through the rumor mill.

<u>Step 2: Research harassment laws and your company's harassment policy.</u> Start your research in your employee handbook to see if your company has an official policy on harassment, discrimination, or bullying. If you don't see anything there, ask your supervisor or an HR representative for a copy of the company's harassment policy. Some smaller companies may not have an official policy, in which case you should research harassment laws at the local, state, and federal level to determine your next steps.

If you work for a large corporation, franchise, or institution like a university, they likely have an overarching harassment policy and internal reporting process, and may even have a dedicated department for addressing these issues. In most cases, you will still want to start the reporting process with your direct supervisor in your location, but knowing the organization's broader rules and resources can both strengthen your position during this conversation and ensure you're following the correct steps.

It's also smart to familiarize yourself with the workplace harassment and discrimination laws in your city or state. Federal employment law is enforced by the EEOC, and applies to any employer, employment agency, or labor union with at least 15 employees or members. Most U.S. states have a separate agency that enforces employment laws on the state level, and in 25 states this includes companies with fewer than 15 employees, while 20 state agencies can investigate grievances older than 180 days. Knowing exactly which laws you're protected by can help you decide how to move forward through the reporting process.

Step 3: Make a good faith effort to resolve the issue directly.
This can be an intimidating and difficult conversation, and preparing first by documenting your experiences and researching your company's harassment policy can help bolster your confidence going into it. Calmly explain the behavior, why it's a problem, and your expectations for their behavior in the future. As with other interactions, thoroughly document this conversation and the other person's response, so you can show this to your supervisor or attorney if the behavior persists and you need to report. A few other tips:

- Skip this step if your harasser is violent, aggressive, or has physically harmed you in the past. A private conversation with a physical abuser can quickly turn dangerous, so if you fear for your physical safety, go straight to reporting to a supervisor.
- If your workplace has an official conflict resolution process, taking advantage of that is often better than a private conversation. For one thing, it provides external documentation of your attempt to resolve the behavior. This also opens up the option of having an impartial mediator who can ensure your safety and prevent the other party from warping or lying about what was said during the conversation.
- Avoid naming names of witnesses or corroborating accounts. This protects those individuals from potential retaliation or

targeting, and also prevents your harasser from attempting to intimidate your witnesses or otherwise control the narrative.

<u>Step 4: Contact an attorney who specializes in employee rights.</u>

If you do need to escalate your report to an outside agency, an employment attorney will be able to guide you through that process. They can also help you clarify whether you have a prosecutable claim of harassment or discrimination under federal or state law, and can give you advice during the reporting process to ensure you don't miss steps or weaken your own position out of ignorance.

Reporting Internally

The first thing you need to decide when reporting is who to report the behavior to. In smaller organizations, your direct supervisor is usually the best (and sometimes the only) person to talk to. Even in companies with dedicated HR departments, your boss is often the best person to talk to about issues with coworkers within the team. When your boss is the person you're reporting, choosing who to report to can take a bit more thought. In the big picture, your choices are to file a report through HR or to talk to another member of the leadership team. Your personal experience within the workplace will dictate which option is better. If your interactions with HR have been positive in the past and the department has a track record of supporting employees, going through that official channel will give you the best chance of a positive outcome. If HR isn't a viable or comfortable option, consider who among the company leadership you trust the most to take action, or who has the most direct authority to find a resolution.

Once you decide who to report to, talk to them as soon as possible. Bring your gathered documentation with you, and prepare what you'll say in advance so you can explain the situation and its impact on you clearly and calmly. You should also be specific about what actions you want to have taken, clearly stating what changes would make you feel the situation had been adequately resolved. It can also help to point out how the behavior is disrupting the broader workplace culture and team productivity, especially if the person you're reporting is a leader or top performer. Again, leave the names of non-involved parties out of this conversation, except in the context of being witnesses who can corroborate your story. For example, if you know a coworker is looking for another job because of your boss' bad temper, you can make the business case that his behavior is causing talent loss without specifying which coworker is contemplating quitting.

Once leadership or HR knows about harassment or discrimination, the company is legally obligated to conduct an investigation. This should include interviewing you, the harasser, and any witnesses, reviewing your documentation, and reviewing company documentation of past reprimands or complaints. After this investigation, they'll decide if harassment occurred, and if so should immediately take steps to prevent it continuing in the future. Regardless of their findings, you should not be punished or experience any kind of different treatment because you filed a report.

Bear in mind, the company is only legally required to take action if the behavior violates federal, state, or local discrimination and harassment laws. In the United States, these include:

- **Title VII of the Civil Rights Act (1964)** prohibiting discrimination against employees or job applicants based on race, color, religion, sex, or national origin.

- **Age Discrimination in Employment Act (1967)** prohibiting age discrimination against those who are 40 and older.
- **Americans with Disabilities Act (1990)** prohibiting discrimination against employees or job seekers with disabilities.

The EEOC can prosecute harassment against the classes protected under these laws, as well as sexual harassment that sets up a Quid Pro Quo situation or creates a hostile work environment. Under the EEOC definition or harassment, it must be intentional, severe, and pervasive or repeated. The exception to this are very serious single incidents, like a physical assault. Even if you're not sure whether the behavior violates federal law, however, it is still worthwhile to file a formal complaint if it is impacting your ability to do your job or creating a physically or psychologically unsafe environment. Employees are protected from retribution for reporting, even if the company finds no harassment occurred, and the behavior may still violate company policies that go beyond the federal definition of harassment.

Continue your documentation through the reporting process. Write down details of your initial report, including the date and time, who you spoke to, and what was discussed during the conversation, and do the same with any follow-up interviews. Keep documenting your interactions with the person you reported, as well, especially if they threaten you or continue to harass you. Hopefully your company takes appropriate action and you won't need to use this information, but if they fail to resolve the issue or you face any retaliation, it will be useful for filing a report with outside agencies.

Other Reporting Options

In the perfect world, every employee grievance would be investigated objectively, and the victims of harassment and discrimination would feel safe and comfortable in their workplace afterwards thanks to the corrective steps their company takes. Unfortunately, in the real world, most workplace harassment doesn't get addressed. In a 2018 survey by Zip Recruiter, only half of those who experienced harassment reported it to their employer. Of those who reported, only 14% of female respondents and 11% of male respondents felt their grievance was fully addressed, while about 20% across genders said their report wasn't addressed at all.

Discrimination, harassment, and bullying are often symptoms of a deeper problem with the organization's culture, and that underlying issue often prevents toxic behavior from being properly addressed. In a fear-based culture, knowing that reporting will lead to a public investigation by the company is enough to deter many victims from making an official grievance, especially against a boss or other authority figure. When reports are made, cliques and workplace politics impair the objectivity of the investigation, and can lead to the victim being ostracized or pushed out of the organization, even if no action is taken that can be litigated as retribution under employment law.

If your workplace is a department, branch, or franchise within a larger corporation, you may be able to escalate your grievance within the company. An increasing number of unions are taking steps to address workplace harassment, so you should check your union contract if you're a union member. Other employee organizations, including unions, professional organizations, and Employee Resource Groups, may be able to connect you with resources like attorneys or contact information for your local EEOC or state employee rights agency, so it's worth it to reach out to these groups if your workplace has them, even if they can't investigate grievances themselves.

Most workers in the United States can file a grievance directly with the EEOC at their local field office, though as we said before, there are restrictions. Those who work for companies that employ fewer than 15 people are not protected under federal employment laws, and that includes workers who are technically self-employed like independent contractors, gig workers, and freelance. The initial conversation is confidential. If they suspect harassment occurred, they will conduct an independent investigation, then work with the company on behalf of the victim to resolve the situation and prevent future harassment.

The majority of U.S. states also have agencies that investigate harassment claims, though there are exceptions. Alabama, Arkansas, Mississippi, and North Carolina lack either state discrimination laws or agencies to enforce them, so in those states it's best to go straight through the EEOC. Georgia's Commission on Equal Opportunity only applies to public employees, while Virginia's agency can only investigate companies that are smaller than 15 employees, so most employees in those states will also want to file grievances with their local EEOC field office. In every other state, though, there is a state-level agency authorized to investigate employers, and as we mentioned earlier in the chapter, many can pursue resolution for cases the EEOC can't investigate, either because the company is too small or the claim is older than 180 days. An employment attorney will know best whether a state agency or the local EEOC field office is the best place to handle your specific claim.

After Reporting

Knowing you are legally protected from harassment and retribution for reporting is all well and good, but legal proceedings can take a long time, and while those go on you still need to work. If you're still facing a hostile environment after exhausting all your avenues of reporting, it's time to decide whether it's worth it to cope with the stress or if it's time to find a new workplace. Assess the long-term impacts on your career and mental health, and whether it's worth it to wait for a resolution, and for how long. When discrimination and hostility have become entrenched in the culture, it's very difficult to change this environment from the employee level, and you don't want to get stuck in an unhealthy situation waiting for improvements that never come.

Chapter 9:

NAVIGATING WORKPLACE FRIENDSHIPS

Having friends at work is by and large a good thing. For one thing, the workplace is a much more enjoyable place to be if you have people you can talk to, joke around with, or confide it. And there is a business case for workplace friendships, too. In a 2021 survey of employees at more than 1,000 companies, 22% of respondents said they're more productive when working alongside a friend, while 21% said it made them feel more creative. Forming a bond with a coworker also makes employees feel more connected to their workplace, building their loyalty to and trust in the organization as a whole. Respondents to GloboForce's Workforce Mood Tracker survey who had friends at work were three times more likely to say they love their company, and 79% said they would reject a job offer from another firm, compared to only 58% of those with no workplace friends.

While most people have made friends at work (95% of the GloboForce respondents), not everyone views these relationships the same way. Researchers at Olivet Nazarene University asked 3,000 U.S. workers to sort their colleagues into categories. Four out of five respondents said they have at least one friend in their current workplace, but they sorted more colleagues into the "only-at-work friends" category (20%) than the "real friends" category (15%). That highlights one potential complication of making friends at work: your colleagues may have different expectations of what a work friendship should be like. Some people thrive when they have a best friend or work spouse a few desks over, while others would rather keep their colleagues as friendly acquaintances. Whatever depth of relationship you prefer, there are some best practices you can follow to ensure that interaction stays positive.

Maintaining Healthy Workplace Friendships

Workplace friendships often form quickly. In the Olivet Nazarene University study, 21% of respondents said their current workplace friendships had formed within a few days of meeting them. This makes sense; most people spend more time with their coworkers than anyone else outside their immediate family (and maybe even more than them). In some cases, the friendship may predate your time as coworkers, such as when a friend or family member refers you for a job or vice versa.

However the friendship formed, there are some simple rules you can follow that will prevent a lot of common issues in workplace friendships.

<u>Rule 1: Establish boundaries.</u>

When you meet new friends outside the workplace, most of the time you don't see them 4-5 days a week. You more likely hang out for a few hours at a time, most likely doing things you both enjoy. This creates a low-pressure environment for you to feel each other out and learn each other's time and space boundaries. There isn't time to form these kinds of organic boundaries in many workplace friendships. Stating them up front can prevent your coworkers from crossing lines they didn't even know were there, and stop you from unintentionally making your new friend feel annoyed or uncomfortable.

Setting boundaries is equally crucial when you start working with someone who is your friend outside the workplace. There may be things you talk about as friends that you would prefer not be discussed around your colleagues. Many people have a professional persona they adopt when they go to work and act, talk, or dress differently than they do around their friends. Boundaries help you define rules for your workplace interactions to prevent misunderstandings or awkward situations.

Introducing these boundaries early helps you present them in a positive way, as part of getting to know each other as coworkers. If they come up later, after a boundary is breached, the conversation is more likely to result is defensiveness, arguments, and negative emotions that can damage the relationship.

<u>Rule 2: Communicate transparently.</u>

There will inevitably be moments when you disagree with friends at work, or they say or do something that bothers you. When this happens, many people's first instinct is to avoid the potential conflict of discussing the issue, but this only leads to potentially bigger conflict in the future. Addressing the source of the disagreement openly and honestly will build a stronger relationship in the long run, one built on mutual respect and understanding rather than assumptions.

While healthy friendships increase feelings of psychological safety, unhealthy behaviors can develop when friends don't communicate openly. Repressed emotions like resentment or jealousy can come out as passive-aggression, gossip, or backstabbing that permanently damage the relationship. It's far better to face the small conflict of bringing these emotions to light as soon as they develop than the more cataclysmic fall-out that can result from ignoring them.

Rule 3: Respect the workplace hierarchy.

The power dynamics and politics of the workplace add a complication to friendships between coworkers that doesn't exist in other contexts. This is especially true when your friend is also your boss, or becomes your boss after the friendship forms. When you are in the workplace context, this power dynamic needs to be respected by both parties. You want to be careful to avoid any activity that looks like favoritism from the outside, as well as any behavior that could feel like either friend is taking advantage of the other.

If you are in a leadership position over a friend, make sure that friendship doesn't influence the projects or feedback they receive. They should get equal praise and critical feedback to any other employee when the situation calls for it. High-profile projects should be assigned based on accomplishments and skill levels, not your personal relationships. On the other side of things, you shouldn't expect your friend to take on extra work or unsavory tasks only as a favor to you, and should respect their workplace boundaries equally to those of your other reports.

For those on the report side of the relationship, avoid putting your friend in situations that create conflict between your friendship and their position. Follow the same rules that apply to everyone else—and, if you do break them, don't expect or ask to be exempt from discipline. Respect your friend's authority when they assign you to teams, tasks, or projects, or when they give you critical feedback. Being friends with the boss can be a great thing for your workplace environment, but you shouldn't see it as something to exploit so you can advance your career.

<u>Rule 4: Be inclusive and considerate with coworkers.</u>

Some people will be naturally drawn to each other more than others, but you want to avoid creating an exclusionary, clique-based culture. A workplace friendship shouldn't prevent you from maintaining cordial relationships with everyone you work with, or make other coworkers feel like they don't belong. When working with friends as part of team projects or collaboration, make sure you give equal attention to everyone's input. If you often eat lunch together, make a point of inviting that shy colleague or new intern, and include them in the conversation if they accept. Your inner circle should be a support system, not a barrier between you and others in your workplace.

In a similar vein, keep your workplace conversations positive, especially when they concern other colleagues. There is a fine line between venting about a workplace frustration and catty gossip that creates a negative work environment. Problems with other coworkers should be addressed with them directly, not discussed behind their back. Even things spoken about in confidence can become fodder for gossip if they're overheard, or allowed to slip in the wrong context. A blanket policy of not gossiping about colleagues is the best way to avoid these kinds of conflicts all together.

<u>Rule 5: Keep work time for work.</u>

One of the biggest potential pitfalls of workplace friendships is that they can become a distraction. On the day-to-day level, this could be time wasted chatting instead of working on a key project. An argument or fall-out with a friend can be an even more significant distraction, especially if it creates a hostile workplace environment.

If you're friends outside of work, one of the things to establish from the beginning is what does and does not belong in the workplace. Leave conversations about things happening in your personal life outside the office, especially if you need to talk about serious or difficult topics that require your full focus. Keep an eye on the clock when chatting with work friends, and if you notice it's cutting into your work time suggest tabling the conversation and meeting up after work to continue it. This can also help ensure you're putting in the effort to maintain your friend relationship outside the workplace.

Maintaining your big-picture focus is important, too. Caring about your friends shouldn't mean neglecting your career progress or workplace goals. You can celebrate their accomplishments and help them with their struggles, but this should be a reciprocal relationship. If you are always putting aside your work to help with theirs and that support never goes the other direction, take a hard look at the friendship and consider redefining the boundaries. You can be a good friend while still thriving as an individual, and the healthiest workplace friendships are built on that foundation.

Red Flags in Workplace Friendships

Workplace friendships overall are a positive and beneficial thing, but that is not to say every single friend relationship in the workplace is a good one. Work friendships can also be destructive and emotionally taxing, and this doesn't only happen when there is an outright conflict. It takes emotional effort to maintain interpersonal relationships, and in some cases, those relationships can be draining, demanding more of this energy than you have to spare.

How can you know when a workplace friendship is unhealthy? Here are some of the most common signs:

- **Things you share in confidence become workplace gossip.** Trust in crucial in any friendship. If your friend is sharing your secrets behind your back, that is a sign they don't have your best interests at heart.

- **Your friend only cares about their accomplishments.** In a balanced friendship, both parties celebrate each other's successes equally, and both of their accomplishments are seen as equally important.

- **You're always solving their problems.** In a similar vein, help and support should flow both directions in a healthy friendship. You may offer friends extra help when they're going through a difficult time (and vice versa), but in the long-term this should balance out.

- **They undermine your successes.** It can be difficult when work friends get the promotions, raises, or accolades you wanted, but sabotaging the other person's progress, consciously or not, isn't a healthy way to deal with those emotions. Your friends should build you up, not tear you down.

There are potential drawbacks to workplace friendships even when they are functioning in a healthy way. Working with close friends can make it more difficult to raise difficult questions or share contrasting opinions. As humans, when we like being around someone we want them to keep liking us back, and will be naturally more hesitant to disagree with or contradict them. That could mean less deliberate and rigorous decision making, and could mean your team isn't considering the best options or exploring all possible solutions to problems. Being mindful of these potential problems will allow you to spot them when they arise, making sure your workplace friendships stay beneficial.

Work Spouses

A special category of workplace friendship is the work spouse relationship. This is a concept already familiar to many—according to a 2017 survey by Captivate, 70% of professionals have a colleague they would call their work spouse. As the term implies, the relationship is very similar to a marriage, only without the romantic parts of the equation. You could also think of it as a work sibling or close best friend, and it describes two people who share strong bonds of mutual trust, support, respect, and loyalty.

The lack of romantic entanglements is crucial for a "work marriage" to function in a healthy way, and the most common way that these relationships go awry. A separate survey from Simply Hired shows how pervasive this issue is. Of their respondents who said they have had a work spouse, 81% of men and 61% of women reported developing romantic feelings. As with other workplace relationships, establishing boundaries from the beginning can help to avoid this kind of sticky situation. For those who have romantic partners, introducing them to the work spouse can help ensure these boundaries stay firm. Having that level of transparency in the relationship can prevent either side from taking the connection too far. Balancing the relationship with other workplace friendships is another smart move, too. This can help prevent either party from relying on the relationship as their sole source of support or only sounding board for their frustrations.

Two other pieces of advice that can help workers navigate a work spouse relationship:

1. Always be mindful of how the relationship looks from the outside. Any close bond formed within a broader group can lead to resentment, or leave others feeling left out. Both

members of the work marriage should be proactive in forming and maintaining other friendships, and avoiding exclusionary behavior, like speaking in inside jokes or gossiping about other coworkers. If you hear rumors about your relationship, be proactive in shutting them down, but also examine your interactions and identify behaviors that might have led to these rumors starting in the first place.

2. Maintain your independence and self-reliance. A close friend in the workplace can be good for your career progress. It means having someone to celebrate your accomplishments and commiserate about your frustrations, ultimately making your work day more enjoyable. However, this kind of relationship can have the opposite effect if the relationship becomes unbalanced. Neither party should be regularly doing the other person's work, or be responsible for the other's success.

Workplace Romance

The complexities and potential complications of workplace friendships are amplified when those relationships turn romantic. This is a large part of why some companies have rules against them—romantic relationships can be messy, especially when they end, and the fall-out from that can affect the team beyond those individuals who were involved in it.

Like friendships, though, it's easy to see why workplace relationships form. And they're not always a bad thing; there are plenty of examples out there of people who met their long-term partner in their workplace, from high-profile celebrities to anecdotal tales among your friends or family. Approaching the romantic relationship carefully and professionally from the beginning is the best way to steer it toward that more positive outcome—or, at the least, to prevent it from affecting anyone's career or workplace comfort.

Before getting involved in a workplace romance, you should check your employee handbook to see what rules the company has on in-office dating. If it's fully banned, you need to decide if the relationship is worth both of you risking your jobs for it, and come up with ground rules to keep the relationship outside the workplace as much as possible. The point of these rules isn't a draconian attempt to control employees' lives—it's to prevent the distraction and disruption a romantic relationship can cause, and you can respect and honor this by avoiding workplace behavior that could distract you or others from your day-to-day tasks. Other workplaces may not ban office romances outright, but have certain rules you need to follow for them to be accepted. These could include disclosing your relationship to supervisors, avoiding dating across hierarchy lines, or ensuring that romantic partners are never put in a position of direct authority over one another. Again, following these rules from your company is the best way to avoid negative consequences that could impact your career.

Aside from these official rules, there are some unspoken guidelines that are smart to follow. First, even if your company allows office romance, be discrete and limit romantic behavior when you're in the workplace. Save your physical affection for outside the workplace. This means no holding hands on the way to work meetings, no stealing kisses by the copy machine, and absolutely no sneaking off to the supply closet for a more intimate moment. Along with helping to prevent the relationship from becoming a distraction for those involved, this also helps you avoid making others in the workplace feel uncomfortable. Similarly, discuss how you'll conduct yourselves if you have a fight or squabble, and put guidelines in place to prevent that disagreement from negatively impacting your work. Conflict is inherently uncomfortable, and your colleagues shouldn't have to have front row seats for all your lover's quarrels. In the same vein, avoid venting about your romantic partner to other colleagues, or sharing private information that could damage their reputation and perception in the company.

Another smart step to take from the beginning is to plan for what you'll do if you break up. A lot of people don't want to think about the potential end of a relationship as it's starting—in those early, love-filled days, it can feel like it was meant to be and is going to last forever. And it well might, but statistically, more romantic relationships end in breakups than marriages, and if that happens you'll be dealing with negative emotions that could prevent you from acting as rationally as you otherwise would. Having a plan for the end of the relationship can help prevent messy fall-out that torpedoes your career, or greatly disrupts the work environment.

As your relationship progresses, it's very important to avoid anything that could be seen as favoritism or bias. This is the main reason most offices ban dating between managers and their reports, but it isn't only a problem across hierarchy lines. In team meetings, make sure you're paying equal attention to everyone in the room, not only listening to your partner. When working on tasks for others, prioritize them fairly based on their actual timeliness or importance, rather than valuing the tasks for your partner over those for other coworkers. While you can't necessarily control how your colleagues view your relationship, you can limit the likelihood they'll see it as unfair or unprofessional by behaving fairly and professionally in all your interactions.

Something else to talk about from the beginning is how you'll ensure that you each maintain your independence and career progress in the workplace. You don't want to reach the point you're thought of as a unit. Each of you should remain a fully separate professional in the workplace context, even if the relationship does evolve into a life-long commitment. Discuss what you'll do if one of you gets promoted while you're together. If the relationship gets serious, it's often smart for one party to take a position at a different company. This will prevent your pairing from negatively impacting either of your career progress—leadership may not consider one of you for a promotion, for example, knowing that you are an "item" and that could lead to an awkward situation, so your being together could be a barrier to advancement in the long term should you stay in the same workplace. Having one of you move to a different department or company can also help prevent your work and personal lives from becoming too intertwined.

The Bottom Line on Work Friendships
Many of the suggestions in this chapter boil down to a similar bullet point: remember that you are at work to work, and everything else you do in the workplace should support you and your colleagues' ability to do that. Workplace friendships can be a powerful support system that makes your workplace a more enjoyable place to be. Maintaining your professionalism and open, transparent communication is the best way to ensure they stay positive, rather than becoming a source of tension and chaos in your workplace.

Chapter 10:
SETTING BOUNDARIES

The word "boundaries" has come up a lot already in the previous chapters—and with good reasons. Healthy boundaries are a necessary component of workplace friendships and are equally important in the employee/manager relationship. They are what maintain your autonomy within the workplace, allowing you to maintain your mental health, physical space, and independent identity during your time at work.

There are many types of workplace boundaries. The easiest to recognize are physical boundaries, which you can otherwise think of as your personal bubble. Physical boundaries determine how much personal space you need to feel comfortable, when and by who you are comfortable being touched, and who is allowed to touch or use your personal possessions or items on your desk. Time boundaries are also very important in the modern workplace, allowing you to regulate how much of your schedule you devote to others, how much you devote to your work, and how much you save for yourself. There are also mental and emotional boundaries, which are the most intangible and most difficult to enforce. These could include the topics you prefer not to discuss in the workplace, or what types of comments and behavior you consider offensive or inappropriate.

Workplace boundaries establish the ground rules for interpersonal interactions. When everyone is able to assert and maintain their boundaries, it reduces the risk of conflicts, hurt feelings, and burn-out, ensuring that all team members feel respected and psychologically safe. Conversely, many of the toxic behaviors and workplace issues discussed in previous chapters can be boiled down to some kind of boundary violation.

Unfortunately, just because boundaries are necessary does not always mean they're easy to establish and assert. Setting firm boundaries can take practice and dedication, as can learning how to respect the boundaries established by your colleagues. This learning process sometimes means unlearning bad habits and making behavioral changes, and that is equally true for the boundary setter as the one they're setting the boundary for. The first step is identifying where you need boundaries, what your personal boundaries are, and how you can communicate those to others.

Finding Your Boundary Lines

Some boundaries are obvious. Often, these stem from your personal values and moral beliefs, and are deeply linked to your personal sense of right and wrong. It is an obvious boundary violation if a coworker, say, steals something off your desk, because this behavior is objectively wrong by most moral compasses. These types of boundaries are also the easiest to enforce since they often violate the broader established rules of either the workplace or society as a whole.

In other cases, boundaries are more subtle, and you may not realize they have been violated until after the fact, sometimes not until it has a negative impact on your work environment or leads you into burnout. For these cases, the best way to identify what boundary has been crossed is to pay attention to your emotions. Pay attention to the people or tasks that make you feel stressed, anxious, or resentful. It may be helpful to keep a workplace journal and jot down what you're doing or who you're interacting with when these feelings come up. Other signs that you need to establish a boundary include:

- <u>You dread an upcoming task, event, or interaction</u>. Dread is a form of anxiety, and feeling it about a commitment or co-worker is a sign of a crossed boundary. Identify what specifically you're dreading to hone in on the exact limits you should set in the future.

- <u>You're always exhausted or can't relax during your off time</u>. Even if you have a passion for your work, nobody wants to think about work all the time. If you feel like you can never truly "sign off", you need to establish a time boundary.

- <u>You're always angry or irritated</u>. It is harder to regulate negative emotions when you are under stress or feel threatened. If you find you get irritated more often or at smaller things than before, consider whether something in the workplace is pushing you past your comfortable limits.

- <u>You feel used or exploited</u>. It is healthy to do things to help out your coworkers, or do a bit extra here and there to impress your boss. This becomes a problem when you allow others to take advantage of you. In some cases, these feelings manifest in a martyr complex, where the individual embraces their role as the victim and refuses solutions that could make their lives easier. An example would be turning down help from coworkers on a large task your boss assigns you at the last minute, even though doing so means you'll have to stay past the end of your shift.

- <u>You're jealous of people who assert their boundaries</u>. Often, this initially comes out as judgment—thinking of someone as lazy because they leave work on time, or saying a colleague isn't a team player because they said no to an extra assignment. Consider whether you really feel that way or if you wish you could follow their lead. When you feel envious of others' boundaries, it is usually because you need more of your own.

Setting boundaries won't fix every workplace issue. When the environment is toxic your boundaries may be habitually ignored even after you state them, and in fear-based cultures you may not feel empowered to state them in the first place. Even in these situations, however, assessing where your boundaries should be, and how violations of them affect your emotions and mental health, can help you find solutions and coping mechanisms.

Setting Boundaries Step-by-Step

For most jobs, part of the orientation process is going through the expectations and behavior standards in the employee handbook. These basic rules establish what is considered acceptable behavior in the workplace, and outline consequences if these rules aren't followed. This is partially to protect themselves from backlash when employees are disciplined or fired for breaking those rules, but it also makes sure new hires understand what the behavior standards are. The more diverse the backgrounds and worldviews in the workplace, the less likely it is they all share the same definition of "acceptable behavior".

Setting boundaries is the same basic concept on the interpersonal level. If you haven't told your managers or coworkers what your limits are, they will be more likely to go past them, and may not even realize that a line has been crossed. Here are some steps to help your colleagues recognize your boundaries, without negatively impacting your work interactions:

1. Decide before the conversation what specific behaviors you want to see changed, and offer an alternative. This makes sure there is no misunderstanding, and gives the boundary violator a positive example of what they should do moving forward, not just what things they should avoid.

2. Express your limits to the boundary violator calmly and confidently. Keep your focus on how the behavior impacts your ability to do your work over how it makes you feel, especially when setting boundaries with a manager. The issue should not be that they hurt your feelings, but that they are negatively impacting your mental healthy, focus, or psychological safety.

3. Establish clear, easy to understand rules. For some boundaries, it may be helpful to add associated cues or signals for co-workers to follow, like that wearing your headphones at your desk means you're busy and can't chat.

4. Give the other person space to share their thoughts or perspective. Especially when you're setting emotional and mental boundaries, hearing the other person's side can help you come to a deeper understanding about your respective personalities and work styles.

5. Be open to compromise, but hold your boundary firm. Some boundaries are black and white, and leave no room for compromise. Others are more flexible, however, and being willing to work with the other person for a compromise can make them more likely to respect your limits in the future. If your

boss bristles when you tell them not to send e-mails after 5pm, a compromise could be that you promise to read these emails first thing your next work day—the boss can still send them and know you will take care of them as soon as you are able, but you are not agreeing to sacrifice your personal time to acknowledge them.

6. Reinforce the boundaries consistently. Your actions need to match your words for your boundaries to be respected. If you continue to respond to violations, your colleagues will learn the limit isn't that serious and will continue to pass it. When that loquacious colleague leans into your cube even though you have your headphones on, don't take them off to chastise the intruder—this only teaches them you will respond to boundary violations. Instead, ignore the intrusion and maintain your boundary and focus, only responding to them verbally if they ignore this cue and continue to interrupt.

Conversations about boundaries are often difficult and uncomfortable, and more so when they're with those above you in the hierarchy. You might find it helps to practice with smaller, low-stakes boundaries so you get comfortable saying no and setting limits. For example, you could say no to an after-work social outing you don't want to attend as a warm up for setting firmer time boundaries with your boss. It can also help to delay your decision when you're asked to take on extra work or otherwise commit your time. Tell the person you need to think about it or check your schedule and you will get back to them later. This takes away the feeling of being "put on the spot" and gives you time to think through your answer in a lower-pressure setting.

Responding to Boundary Violations

Even with clear communication and firm reinforcement, some people may still cross your boundaries, either knowingly or accidentally. Prepare in advance how you'll respond when this happens so you're ready to address it in the moment when it happens. Boundary reminders are another opportunity to teach your coworkers the best ways to communicate with you and when it's appropriate to do so. Getting pushback on the boundary is a sign it's necessary, so don't let coworker violations undermine the process. Be kind and respectful but firm when asserting boundaries. The type of boundary and how it's violated will determine the best response. While you want to address these violations promptly, sometimes it's best to not respond in the moment when the boundary is one of time, as we mentioned above. If your boss emails late at night again after you've told them not to, sending any response—even a negative one—reinforces their boundary-breaking behavior. In this case, a prompt response would be to talk to them about it during your next shift.

If your boundaries are still repeatedly disregarded after you have had a conversation and made efforts to reinforce them, this tells you there is a deeper problem with toxicity and employee autonomy in your workplace. When this is the case, the healthiest option is to look for a new job where your limits and preferences will be respected. In the mean time, there are some tips you can follow to lessen the impact of boundary violations on your mental health:

- <u>Embrace saying no</u>. This is certainly easier said than done in professional contexts, but is a crucial skill for boundary setting, especially boundaries related to time and space. The good news is, it gets easier the more you do it. While you shouldn't need to explain yourself, doing so can help when you are saying "no" to a manager or leader. This could mean pointing out your already full schedule when they try to add work to it, or explaining what is and is not in your job description if they ask you to take on assignments you lack the skills, training, or resources for.

- <u>Delegate</u>. Delegating isn't only a skill for managers. If you are asked to take on work outside your responsibilities, suggesting someone who may be better for the job is a softer way to decline it, and can help in conversations with stubborn boundary-defying managers. You can also take a similar approach when invited to events or social outings, declining the invite but suggesting they extend it to another colleague you think would enjoy the opportunity, or at least have time to take part in it.

- <u>Use technology to your benefit</u>. The 24/7 connectivity of the modern world is a big reason many of us need firmer boundaries today than in the past, but technology can also be helpful when establishing your limits. Creating automatic replies or status updates for when you aren't available can be a good way to reinforce time boundaries in the moment without breaking them yourself. Scheduling and task management tools are a place you can share your work hours with colleagues so they know when you are available and when you're not. Many programs and devices have "Do Not Disturb" modes or similar settings that block notifications during certain times of the day, while social media platforms and similar programs often have settings for blocking individual accounts from messaging you or seeing your posts. Using these tools can help maintain your boundaries even when colleagues or managers fail to respect them.

- <u>Get help from your allies</u>. Your workplace friends and co-workers who do understand boundaries can help you reinforce them with chronic boundary violators. Mentors and colleagues may also be able to offer advice on ways they have set boundaries you may not have thought of.

The Value of Boundaries

There is a misconception that boundaries limit interpersonal connections. In reality, the opposite is true. Boundaries strengthen relationships by ensuring both parties feel comfortable, safe, and respected, leading to healthier, more sustainable interactions. A lack of boundaries, meanwhile, results in misunderstandings, resentment, and overwork, all of which impair employees' productivity and mental health. At the leadership level, encouraging and enabling your team to set their own boundaries (and respect those of others) helps to build a healthier, more communicative team environment that allows everyone to be their full, best selves.

Chapter 11:
GETTING AHEAD (WITHOUT BURNING BRIDGES)

Getting a promotion is good news, but like any change it can lead to unintended consequences. The people you thought were your friends or allies may turn distant or even hostile out of jealousy, resentment, or uncertainty about how the new power dynamics will impact your friendship. For some, workplace politics can be a barrier to taking advantage of advancement opportunities, especially if your organization has issues with bias or favoritism.

There are no easy answers for how to balance career progress with your workplace relationships and environment. In some cases, changing companies will be the smoothest and easiest option for advancing through hierarchy levels, while others will prefer to stay with their current company and need strategies to maintain pre-existing friendships after moving up the corporate ladder. In this chapter, we'll look at some strategies for identifying and seizing advancement opportunities without disrupting your workplace relationships.

Moving Your Career Forward

Ideally, the process to advance your career should be, if not easy, at least straightforward. Unfortunately, in the real world that is not always the case. Many companies lack a clear promotion policy, and lack of clarity regarding workplace expectations or job responsibilities can make it difficult for employees to even gauge where they stand with their immediate manager, much less in the eyes of the broader leadership team. Even well-defined career pathways can become clouded when bias, favoritism, and workplace politics come into play. All of this can leave employees feeling confused and frustrated, and make applying for a job with another company seem like the only option when they want to push their career to the next level. That may well be the best option for some, but before you embark on the work of a job search, there are some steps you can take within your current company to help you move forward.

The first step is to figure out what you ultimately hope to achieve. Do you have a specific position or hierarchy level in mind as your end goal, or do you just want to take on more responsibility (and the higher paycheck that comes with it)? Taking the time to lay out a tentative five- or ten-year plan can help you clarify what skills you need to focus on and which types of positions will be the best move. This may not always mean going up the corporate ladder. A lateral shift into a position that gives you a more diverse skill set, or opens up more advancement opportunities, may be the best move for some. It can be helpful to talk to someone who is a few steps further down your ideal career path to find out how they got to where they are. While those who work in your industry will be able to give you the most specific, actionable advice, talking to a more general mentor can still give you helpful insights about how to move forward.

Once you know what position or role you want to move into, you can better assess whether that can be accomplished within your company or if you need to seek a new environment. Talk to your boss about your goals and what options exist for getting you closer to them. Even if there aren't open positions at the moment, there may be professional development or upskilling opportunities that can get you started, or you could take on added responsibilities that complement your current role, expanding your skills (and bolstering your resume) so you can be ready when there is an opening. If you can't or don't want to talk to your boss about this for whatever reason, you can also have this conversation with HR, or another member of your company's leadership—anyone who has access to employee development resources and understands the hiring and promotion policies in your workplace. The bottom line is that you want to make your interest in advancement known to the people who can help you do it, and even better if they're involved in making those decisions.

Another great way to identify what skills you will need to move your career forward is to hit the job boards. Compare the requirements and responsibilities on a few different posts to identify the most desirable qualifications and experience, then read your resume and CV through that lens. As you move forward, keep track of your successes related to those areas. It can help to have a folder (be it physical or digital) where you save records of your accomplishments like sales figures, positive feedback from customers or clients, or copies of performance reviews and workplace accolades. At the same time, identify the skills or experience that you are missing, and take steps to fill in those gaps through certifications or the projects you take on in the workplace.

For some, an unclear path to advancement is only one of the barriers between them and their career progress. Structural or leadership bias can prevent employees from being fairly considered. It is very difficult to position yourself for advancement when your boss plays favorites, fails to acknowledge employee accomplishments, or steals credit for your work. In a hostile work environment, behaviors like gossip, backstabbing, blame, and sabotage can mar the victim's record and reputation, making it equally difficult to get ahead. While the healthiest option in these cases is often to find a new job, there are steps you can take to maintain your forward momentum despite the bias or toxicity in your work environment:

- <u>Show your work</u>. It is especially important to keep track of your accomplishments when you are the target of bias or credit-stealing. Sharing this information can also help you get due credit for your work. If a colleague regularly fails to give you credit for joint assignments, for example, CC-ing the boss when you send along work and updates can ensure your contributions are acknowledged.

- <u>Partner with allies to amplify each other's ideas and accomplishments</u>. Talk to your friends and allies in the workplace about ways you can actively support each other against bias, exclusion, or favoritism. When your allies share ideas in team meetings and collaborations, second them while giving your colleague credit, and ask them to do the same to you. The same approach can be used with reports or project updates if another colleague tries to diminish you or an ally's role, or take credit for the ideas and work of others. The more voices are giving credit where it is due, the harder they are to ignore.

- <u>Don't give in to negative emotions</u>. Feeling angry and frustrated is natural when someone ignores your hard work (or claims it as their own), but if you let these emotions take over, you are only hurting yourself. Only speak up in the moment if you can do so calmly. Otherwise, take time to process your emotions before you decide how to address the situation. While you should push back when you are treated unfairly in the workplace, reacting out of anger can reflect poorly on you and undermine your career progress.

If you do decide your best way forward is to change companies, make sure your work quality stays high after you make that decision. Stay engaged with your coworkers, clients, and projects so that your most recent work will be a true reflection of your capability. Once you find a new role, have a personal conversation with your work friends about your decision to move on, and put in the effort after you change companies to maintain those professional connections. The broader your network, the more likely you will be to hear about opportunities in the future. Even if you had an overall negative experience at a company it is to your benefit to leave on good terms, especially with those colleagues who did support you during your time there.

The Human Side of Success

Most people want their friends to be successful—but it can still sting when they get promotions or accolades you wanted for yourself. Workplace relationships can also be strained when individuals move up through the hierarchy and power dynamics shift. Those you were close to as a coworker may not know where they stand when you become their boss, and the manager who supported you as a report could see you as a threat if you rise quickly once you become their peer.

Jealousy is at the root of a lot of negative workplace behaviors. Colleagues who resent being passed over for a promotion or award will often take that out on the person who received it. Some common signs of jealousy in the workplace include:

- Mocking other people when they get recognition
- Exclusion from social gatherings, conversations, or meetings and collaboration sessions
- Snide comments about the other person's work
- Spreading gossip and rumors
- Always contradicting or disagreeing with what the other person says
- Backstabbing or sabotage

If you notice one or more of these behaviors from coworkers after you get a big raise, promotion, or make other career progress, jealousy is likely to blame. So what should you do about it? As long as it isn't impacting your ability to do your job, the best option is to ignore it. Most likely, their jealousy will fade with time and you can rebuild your old friendly relationship; focus your energy on maintaining and building friendships with coworkers who support your success in the mean time. If their behavior is impacting your work, talk to them directly about the behavior, how it is affecting you and the broader workplace, and how you can improve your interactions moving forward.

There are also some strategies you can employ to prevent jealous reactions from coworkers and mitigate its impact when it does occur:

1) <u>Share the spotlight</u>. This doesn't mean to give others credit for work you did, but instead elevating the work of others alongside yours. Give due credit to any collaborators or helpers when you're congratulated for successes, and make a point of celebrating the accomplishments of your colleagues as they

happen. If you are a cheerleader for others' successes, they'll be less likely to resent yours.

2) <u>Use your rise in status to help others</u>. As you rise in status or position, don't forget where you started and the people who helped you along the way. Talk up your coworkers to new allies you form in upper hierarchy levels, and suggest them for projects or opportunities you hear about that could further their careers.

3) <u>Stay open to learning from your colleagues</u>. It's healthy to be proud of your accomplishments, but no matter how high you climb, there is always more to learn. People who act like they know everything are more likely to attract resentment from colleagues, and this mindset shuts you off from gaining new skills or knowledge that can help you in the future.

4) <u>Save your bragging for the right moments</u>. There are some situations where you want to talk up your accomplishments, like networking events or meetings with leadership and clients. If your coworkers are already jealous, though, hearing you talking about your accomplishments won't help. Be selective in when and how you discuss promotions, raises, and other workplace wins, and be gracious and modest when they're brought up by colleagues.

5) <u>Don't apologize for your success</u>. Downplaying your success or achievement around those who didn't get it just reinforces their resentment—if even you think you're unworthy, that justifies their feeling that the situation is unfair. You can be modest and still own your success and the work you did to earn it.

6) <u>Share your knowledge</u>. You want to be careful with this one. Offering unsolicited advice can come across as arrogant, or

like you're looking down on the recipient. When asked to share advice, though, be forthcoming with any strategies you used or insider tips you're able to pass along.

Navigating work relationships as you progress through your career can be complicated, and there are no hard and fast rules for doing it successfully. Some work friendships may fade as you advance despite your best efforts. You can't control how other people feel, only the way you respond to it. Keep your side of interactions calm and positive, and focus your energy on the people who root for your success, not the ones who want to undermine it. If a former friend starts giving you the cold shoulder or spreading rumors about you, take a second to step back and understand their motivation before you confront them. The behavior likely has more to do with their insecurities than it does with you, so while it can hurt to feel betrayed or rejected by a one-time friend, try not to take it personally. Ultimately, it's a compliment when someone feels threatened by your success, and looking at the situation through that lens can help you keep your cool in these frustrating situations.

Chapter 12:
STUCK IN THE MIDDLE

In 2014, *Harvard Business Review* conducted an analysis of more than 320,000 employees to assess their relative levels of engagement and workplace satisfaction. Those in the lowest 5%—in other words, the least engaged and most disgruntled of the respondents—were, by and large, not overworked executives or underpaid entry-level talent. The majority of these low engagement scores came from the middle of the hierarchy: those who had been with their company 5-10 years and served as middle managers within their organization's structure. In a similar vein, a 2015 study by researchers from Columbia University found mid-level managers have the highest rates of depression and anxiety compared to other hierarchy levels.

For those who work as middle managers, these findings are not surprising. Middle managers are in a uniquely challenging position because they serve as both followers and leaders. This gives them a complicated relationship with workplace power. They're expected to be assertive and in charge when interacting with reports, but to take a more deferential attitude with their superiors. Switching between these modes throughout their workday adds stress and tension to the workplace dynamic. It's a form of code-switching, not unlike the tension created for professionals from under-represented groups who feel the need to speak and act differently in the workplace than they do in their day-to-day life. This is exacerbated by the fact that the demands placed on middle managers are often in conflict. They're the ones who implement the strategies and changes outlined by upper leaders, balancing them against the needs of their reports. In ideal workplaces these naturally align, but in the real world that is often not the case.

Some challenges of being a mid-level leader are inherent to the role and cannot be avoided entirely. On the plus side, small adjustments at the organizational and upper leadership level can greatly reduce the stress level of middle managers. And it behooves organizations to make these changes. In a large-scale analysis of the computer game industry by Wharton's Ethan Mollick, the behavior of middle management accounted for 22.3% of the revenue variance between companies. Middle managers have an equally large impact on organizational culture. They have the most direct influence on employees' day-to-day lives and are situated at the pivot point between the top and bottom of the hierarchy, serving as the translator of executive ideas and vision into actionable policies and strategies. Understanding what causes anxiety in mid-level managers, and how they impact the work environment and bottom line, is the first step to making changes that will benefit the entire organization.

Why Is Middle Management So Stressful?
Many jobs have aspects that can make them stressful. Those in middle management, though, experience pressure and demands from more directions and sources than those in other areas of the workplace, and that is a significant reason these positions are more consistently more draining for the mental energy and health of those that fill them.

While every workplace is unique, here are the most common sources of stress for mid-level managers and ways those pain points can be avoided.

<u>They feel powerless.</u>
Often, middle managers are expected to carry out executive policies but have no influence or voice in the planning stages of those changes. This lack of agency can leave them in a very difficult situation when the edicts from above are unrealistic. Employees look to their direct managers to explain and justify executive decisions, and that is difficult to do when they are kept in the dark about the c-level's decision-making process and motivation, especially if they disagree with the decision, too. It's frustrating when managers see how ineffective or inefficient policies can be improved, but are ignored when they suggest changes (or not given space to suggest the changes in the first place).

The middle management perspective can be very valuable for upper-level decision makers. They know their team's strengths, capabilities, and motivators, providing practical context for how big-picture ideas will translate into real-world logistics. They have the best view of the gap between the current reality and the desired change, a perspective that is necessary for enacting policies to connect them. If you were building a physical bridge, an obvious first step would be measuring the distance between the two sides and where the structure will need support to keep it standing. It would be foolish to blindly start building the bridge from one side without this information, but that's exactly what upper leaders are doing when they ignore middle manager input. Worse is when executives micromanage mid-level leaders, dictating how strategies should be enacted to the point they feel their hands are tied and they have no power to influence policies.

More transparent and open communication between leadership levels is the first step to reducing this source of stress. A simple change like inviting feedback from middle managers on proposed changes can go a long way. Upper-level leaders should invite this input before decisions have been finalized, working with middle managers to set expectations, deadlines, and benchmarks that are realistic and mutually agreeable. Once decisions are made, upper leaders need to trust their middle managers and give them the freedom to implement strategies the way they think is best. Remember that this individual was put in a leadership position for a reason. Removing agency from middle managers lessens their overall authority, weakening their ability to hold reports accountable and effectively manage their teams. Conversely, giving them influence in the decision-making process increases their ownership in company decisions, empowering them to truly serve as leaders for their teams and restoring their sense of purpose and value, something that's often lacking for those in mid-management roles.

<u>Lack of proper training and clear expectations.</u>
Leading other people requires a unique set of skills. Even those who are naturally inclined to taking charge benefit from training in conflict resolution, delegation, coaching, and other crucial skills for exceptional leadership. Developing these skills is also necessary for middle managers to continue upwards in the hierarchy, yet they are often omitted from new manager training. Instead, individual managers are expected to develop these skills through trial and error, leading to mistakes and missteps that impede the manager's performance and career progress, as well as negatively impacting their teams.

More thorough management training, combined with ongoing coaching and mentorship, is the solution for this problem. It also helps clarify the behavior that is expected from them in their new role. One major source of unhappiness for middle managers is feeling stuck in their role and not seeing a path to promotions or career advancement. Often, the feedback they receive is results-based, with little to no input on their management approach or techniques—they are only told the problems, not guided on how to fix them. Ongoing coaching provides this guidance, while more robust initial training highlights the crucial skills and areas they should focus on from the start. Together, this ensures they are able to develop as leaders.

<u>They are overwhelmed and overworked.</u>
Along with their own workload, middle managers are frequently the first ones called upon to help with others' emergencies and crises. They are where individual contributors go with their issues, the ones called in to resolve client or customer problems, and the target of upper leadership demands and ire. Prioritizing these sources of pressure can be difficult, and leaves little time to take care of themselves and their own work.

Better manager training and clearer expectations will help alleviate this issue. Middle managers are better able to prioritize the many demands on their time when they are given clear guidelines on what roles they are expected to serve. Learning better delegation skills can also clear some of that work off of their plate, allowing them to better identify which tasks they need to do directly and which can be done just as well by others.

Better two-way communication is beneficial here, as well. Often, middle managers feel unable to say no when a superior assigns them a task they simply don't have time for. Open communication between leadership levels lets upper leaders track the workload of their middle managers so they know who has time for an urgent request and who will be overwhelmed if yet another task is vying for their attention. From the other side, empowering managers to say no to projects they lack capacity for gives them tools to better manage their own workload. This, in turn, makes them more effective in their role. When middle managers are over-stressed, that stress trickles down through the rest of the team. They're not able to be as helpful for reports, and are less likely to respond with empathy and compassion when employees or customers come to them with problems. Managers who are given at least some agency over their own workload are able to be better leaders because they have the mental energy to lead with empathy.

<u>They navigating conflicting social expectations.</u>
The rules for appropriate behavior and social interactions change depending on whether you are interacting with someone above or below you in the hierarchy. Those at the upper and lower ends only have to engage in one social mode, but those in the middle have to switch from follower to leader as they navigate their work day. The more frequently they have to shift, and the more strict the lines of power and authority are, the more this drains their mental energy.

This is one of those stressors that is inherent to the middle manager role, but there are ways to minimize the impact of that stress on individuals. Generally, managers in organizations with a more democratic culture are less impacted by this "vertical code-switching" because the difference in professional behavior standards is less pronounced. Conversely, it is most taxing for those in organizations with strict hierarchy delineations. In these cases, reducing the power discrepancy between leadership levels can ease the social stress felt in the middle.

Another strategy here is to cut down on the number of switches between upward and downward interactions. This could mean restructuring the day of middle managers to have their meetings with upper leaders condensed into the start or end of their day, or eliminating unnecessary meetings that force them to make these mental shifts. When meetings are necessary, having a clear agenda in advance allows those in attendance to prepare what they'll say and how much they'll likely be expected to contribute, reducing the anxiety they'll feel going into the interaction.

Navigating Middle Management

Organizations and upper leaders have a lot of power to set their middle managers up for success, but there are also some strategies you can take as a mid-level leader to overcome the challenges of these roles. Here are some best practices and steps to maximize your effectiveness as a mid-level leader:

- **Know your team.** The better you understand what kind of support your reports need, the more efficiently you can provide it, without wasting your time and effort providing help they don't need. Find out what motivates your team, what frustrates them, and where they want or need guidance from their manager. Each individual you manage is likely to have their own opinions on this, so take the time to learn their work styles and preferences so you can better allocate your time and coaching.
- **Work with your boss, not around them.** Just like middle managers support their reports, upper leaders should give similar guidance to those in the middle. Communicate with your

bosses to ensure your goals and visions are aligned. If you don't understand your expectations, ask for clarification. When you feel executives lack understanding about employee needs, tell them so, and provide an alternate solution if you have one. An open and healthy relationship between middle and senior leaders is critical for the organization's success, and while upper leaders have a responsibility to facilitate that open dialogue, middle managers should also be proactive in asking for and providing feedback.

- **Know your abilities, priorities, and management style.** Effective leaders are self-aware, and that's as true for middle managers as it is for executives. It can help to perform a 360° assessment, gathering feedback from your reports, peers, and superiors to identify what you do well and where you can improve.

- **Trust reports to make their own decisions.** Increasing employee agency allows managers to use their time more effectively. The more empowered your reports are to make their own decisions, the less they rely on you for approval, guidance, and motivation. Ensure all team members have the tools, knowledge, and space to do their jobs, and encourage them to take ownership over team and individual goals by welcoming their input in the decision-making process.

- **Amplify understanding through clear communication.** As a leader, you never want to assume that reports understand expectations, roles, processes, and deadlines. Instead, you should clearly spell these out, then ask follow-up questions to ensure your reports fully understand. Taking a few minutes at the start of a task or project to confirm that everyone is on the same page saves you time in the long run because there will be fewer mistakes, missed deadlines, and other metaphorical fires to put out down the line.

- **Establish a support system.** Mid-level management can feel very isolating because you cannot fully relate to either reports or leaders. Cultivate workplace relationships with other middle managers who have faced similar struggles and can offer advice or solutions to the unique problems of the position. It can also help to have a mentor who has been through the trials of middle management and can share first-hand advice for both moving your career forward and tackling the day-to-day issues middle managers encounter.

- **Build your team thoughtfully.** Mid-level leaders are often the main gatekeepers in an organization because they make hiring and disciplinary decisions for individual contributors. This power can be used for good or ill, and a biased or incompetent manager can have a very detrimental effect on the team's inclusivity and overall culture. When hiring, actively seek out individuals that will fill in your team's blind spots and reinforce the ideal culture, creating a team with diverse skill sets and perspectives. A strong, well-trained team means less work for its leader since they can be trusted to complete work delegated to them. All of that starts with effective hiring and training.

Maintaining Work/Life Balance as a Middle Manager

In management, as in many areas of life, the oxygen mask theory applies. If you aren't aware of this analogy, it comes from airline safety videos that tell passengers, in the event of a crash, they should put on their own oxygen mask before assisting others. Put in a team management context, you cannot provide proper support for your team if you are struggling to get through your day-to-day. Maintaining a healthy work/life balance isn't just important for your own mental health, but also a crucial leadership skill, especially in the modern age of 24/7 connectivity.

The many pressures and conflicting demands placed on middle managers can quickly drive them to burn-out if they don't take proactive steps to safeguard and monitor their own mental health. First and foremost, you need to know your non-negotiable boundaries, communicate these to both reports and leaders, and hold them firm on an everyday basis. Middle managers can often be some of the worst violators of their own boundaries. Don't work through breaks or past your established work hours, even if that means pushing tasks to the next day. You can avoid this temptation by being realistic when you schedule your time. Work in some leeway for inevitable interruptions, and establish a system with reports and leaders so they know when you are and aren't available. One approach could be having set "office hours" during the day when reports know they can come to you for coaching or to ask non-urgent questions. Utilize technology in your favor by activating auto-responses on your inbox, text messages, and other communication platforms when you're not working, or working on a task that requires your full focus. If you find you still have more to do than hours in your day after taking these measures, consider which tasks can be delegated to other members of the team, or have a conversation with your boss about reducing your workload.

This leads to the second tip: as a mid-level manager, you need to learn when and how to say no. Effective time management and scheduling makes this easier. Knowing exactly how much time you need for the work you already have means you can realistically assess whether you can fit another project or meeting. It also makes it easier to decline extra work confidently if you can respond to pushback by outlining exactly where your time is currently allocated.

Finally, stay tuned in to your emotions and stress levels. At the start of each work day, take a few minutes to check in with yourself and how you feel about your current workload. When you feel anxiety, dread, or frustration, identify the root of the emotion and find strategies to eliminate any chronic or recurring stressors. Remember, you need to be in a good place mentally, emotionally, and professionally to be best for your team. Resist the temptation to sacrifice your mental health for the "greater good" of your team's needs. Sometimes, the best thing you can do for yourself and your reports is taking a vacation that allows you to refresh and recharge, even if that might seem counterintuitive. There is no secret recipe to surviving as a middle manager, but a few small changes on the personal and organizational level can make a big difference in their ability to thrive.

Chapter 13:
SHOULD I STAY OR SHOULD I GO?

For most of this book, we have looked at ways to improve, or at least cope with, difficult and toxic workplaces. In some cases, however, these methods will not be enough to create a healthy and safe environment where you can thrive long-term. When setting boundaries, open communication with colleagues, and reporting problems to HR or your manager don't solve the problem (or even make it worse), it may be time for you to move on and find a work environment that supports you so you can reach your career goals.

This doesn't always have to mean embarking on a full job search to change companies. When the issues stem from individual managers or coworkers, a change of environment within your current organization can improve your day-to-day workplace without the stress and uncertainty of changing jobs. For others, a fresh start with a new company is the better move, particularly if you are facing systemic bias or working in an organization with toxic upper leadership.

How do you know if it's time to quit—and, if so, how to do it without losing the professional connections you've made in your current role? Let's start by taking a closer look at the first question.

Signs It's Time to Move On

Everyone has bad days at work. Even if you are passionate about your work and invested in your company, there will be times that your job is frustrating, stressful, or just plain boring. The first step to deciding whether it's time to quit is to do some self-analysis. Identify the source of your stress or discontentment as objectively and honestly as you can. It can help to keep a journal during a typical work week. Record the moments you feel negative emotions like dread, anxiety, or anger, along with the situation that led to them and the individuals involved. This can help you to clarify the specific source of the negativity.

Next, analyze those sources of workplace stress and assess the scope of the problem. If the entire organization is inefficient and ineffective, suffering from poor leadership, or runs according to biased or toxic policies, there likely isn't much you can do to change this as an individual team member. On the other hand, if the majority of the issues can be traced back to the behavior of an individual colleague or manager, you may be able to make smaller changes that give you a more sustainable future within the organization.

While every situation is unique, there are some common signs that it is time to make some kind of a change. These include:

- **The job is affecting your physical health.** If you are suffering from chronic pain, insomnia, and stress-related symptoms like headaches, body aches, or more frequent illness, your current job is unsustainable in the long-term.
- **The job is interfering with your family or personal life.** Balancing your career with your personal life can be tricky even in a healthy workplace. That said, if you are routinely asked to sacrifice your free time or life outside of work for the sake

of the company, this is a sign leadership doesn't respect and value the work/life balance of its employees, and you should consider seeking employment elsewhere.

- **You feel overwhelmed and dread going to work.** Even when work isn't necessarily fun, you should feel comfortable with your work environment and job expectations. When every new task is a source of anxiety, this is a sign you are on a path to burnout. Setting firmer time boundaries within your current job may be a solution, but if those are ignored the best solution is to find a work environment with more realistic expectations that allows you to maintain a reasonable workload.

- **Leadership is controlling, untrustworthy, or hostile.** Lack of transparency or outright deceit from leadership makes it difficult to do your job effectively, while micromanagement and other controlling tendencies can prevent you from doing it to your full potential. This not only creates a stressful work environment but impedes your career progress because you aren't able to excel.

- **You are the target of bias or marginalization from leadership.** This could be your direct supervisor or higher leadership—anyone with gatekeeper power over assignments and promotions. If you're being pushed into the background despite your attempts to stand out and advance, it's time to work for a team where your contributions will be valued and seen, even if that marginalization is the unintentional result of sloppy management or poor organizational leadership.

- **You have to compromise your values or ethics.** While your personal values don't need to align perfectly with your company's, the discrepancy between them should never force you to compromise your ethics and morals. If you are being asked to do things that are illegal or unethical, this can reflect poorly on you in the future if those behaviors come to light, so your best option is to remove yourself from that situation as quickly as possible.

- **You are overqualified and have no room to grow.** It's frustrating to feel like your talents aren't being fully utilized, and staying in that kind of position can prevent you from making career progress. When you have reached the top of the ladder for your skillsets within the company, or are routinely turned down or overlooked for new opportunities, it is time to look for an environment where you can make forward progress.

- **The company's future is in question.** It's impossible to build a future with a company if the business fails. Signs of an impending business failure include sweeping layoffs, reductions in the client base, closing offices or locations, and salary freezes. If you sense the business may be in danger of closing, do a bit of digging into their profit and loss records to gauge their long-term financial health. A struggling business will not be able to offer the same opportunities and growth as one that's thriving, so it's often better to leave on your own terms than to wait for the situation to improve.

- **You aren't able to fulfill your job responsibilities.** Sometimes, you need to move on from a position for your own reasons, even if the company and position are suitable. If chronic health conditions, family changes, or other external forces are preventing you from doing your job, consider whether a different career or type of position would be more sustainable. If you stay in the position and your work quality suffers this can limit your opportunities in the future more than an employment gap or career change.

- **You are significantly undercompensated.** Slight variations in pay rate between companies (or even individual team members) are natural in any industry. That said, if you could make significantly more working for a different company, consider what value you are gaining by staying.

Alternatives To Quitting

If one or more of the signs outlined above sounds familiar, odds are good you need a new work environment. As we said before, however, this doesn't necessarily need to mean finding a new company. There are some smaller-scale changes you can make that may resolve the problem entirely, or at the very least reduce their impact on your day-to-day life while you search for better opportunities.

First of all, take a break. A bit of distance and time away from the workplace can help you clarify your feelings about the company and your position within it. If you have PTO saved up it's time to use it, especially if it's been a year or longer since your last vacation. For those considering a career change due to burnout, using your PTO on a more regular schedule is one change that can help you thrive long-term, especially if in conjunction with setting firmer time boundaries and working smaller breaks into your weekly schedule. During this break, think back over your career and why you started this job in the first place. What did you enjoy about the work when you started, and what has changed in either the work itself or how you perceive it to lead to your current dissatisfaction? What were your goals when you accepted this position, what are your current goals, and how does your current workplace help you to meet those? Reconnecting with your passion and career objectives can help you plot out logical, productive next steps, rather than acting out of exhaustion or desperation.

Once you have identified the specific sources of dissatisfaction, go through each one and pinpoint what would need to change in your current work environment to resolve them. There may be options you haven't explored that could improve your situation without the stress and uncertainty of a new job search. If your salary is too low, set up a meeting with your boss to ask for a raise, or discuss other positions or responsibilities you can take on that would increase your value and payrate. Similarly, if a lack of growth or learning opportunities is the issue, explore professional development and reskilling opportunities offered by your company, or talk to your manager about taking on more challenging or varied assignments.

The same advice stands if you feel overwhelmed or need a better work/life balance. Workplace flexibility is an increasingly in-demand benefit, so a strict 9-5 may not be your only option. If your company employs remote or hybrid workers, consider whether that format would give you the flexibility you need, and if so ask your boss if you can switch to that model. Maybe a 4-day work week would be a better fit for your lifestyle, or you could shift your schedule hours earlier or later. The bottom line is, if you see a possible solution, discuss it with someone who has the power to make the change—don't assume their answer will be no before you even ask.

Be honest with yourself about what adjustments you personally can make to your behavior or perspective that could improve your situation, too. Have you set firm boundaries and made legitimate effort to maintain them? If you feel your workload is too much (or, on the other side, not challenging enough) have you discussed that with your boss? Even an empathetic leader cannot read their reports' minds and may not realize you are struggling if you have a tendency to suffer in silence. Similarly, if your work environment is hostile because of conflicts with coworkers, make a concerted effort to improve those relationships. Even if you ultimately do quit, putting in this effort ensures you leave on the best possible terms, and the practice working through workplace conflicts can help you prevent similar issues from occurring in the future.

In some cases, you may feel like you are being forced out of the organization. This can happen because of a specific event, like a bad performance review, or because of recurring interactions, like ostracization from coworkers or frequently having your contributions ignored. Before acting on these feelings, ensure you're interpreting the situation correctly. If you feel you aren't living up to your boss' expectations, have a candid conversation with them about where they want to see improvement, and work with them to set actionable goals with clear benchmarks for progress. The next time a coworker leaves you off an invite list, or talks over you in a meeting, address the issue with them directly one-on-one. Taking action restores your agency. You may still decide to quit, but it will be your decision, not the result of someone else's actions and behavior.

Quitting Like A Pro: Step By Step

You have analyzed your situation and career aspirations and have decided that it is time to quit your job. Just making that decision can be very liberating, and you may be tempted to run straight to your boss and put in your two weeks—but, before you do, there are a few more things you should do and plan to set yourself up for future success. Here are some steps that can help you to quit like a professional.

<u>1) Assess your finances.</u>

Ideally, you'll find a new job right away and won't have to survive long with income coming in. In reality, however, job searches can take a while. Planning ahead financially can prevent you from taking a job out of desperation, giving you the freedom to be picky about what position you take next and making it more likely you'll find a job that's an actual improvement over your current role.

To start, write up a budget of your current monthly expenses. Next, look at this list and cross off anything that is a work-related expense. This could include commuting costs, work clothes and dry-cleaning expenses, and the cost of your daily lunches or morning coffee run. It also includes services you use because you work long hours, such as house cleaning services or dinner delivery, or self-soothing expenditures like massages or alcohol—things you buy to help you cope with your stressful job, but can do without after you quit.

Another smart step to take is to assess your current debt, and whether you can reasonably pay any of it off within the next few months. This can knock another significant expense off of your budget, and prevent you from going into further debt, or needing to choose which expenses you can keep up with, if your job search takes longer than you anticipate.

Now that you have your streamlined monthly expenses, multiply them by six. That is the amount you should have saved up before you quit without another job lined up. If it takes less than six months to find your new job, great—you can use that extra savings for your next vacation, or shift it into your rainy day fund. It's better to have too much saved up and not need it than to find yourself out of money in the middle of your new job search.

<u>2) Re-read your employment contract and benefits information.</u>

For most, salary is just one aspect of their compensation package through their work. Before deciding your next steps, review your initial offer letter and benefits information. Make sure you are past the vesting date for benefits like pensions and stock options, and what will happen to them when you change companies. In some cases you can keep your 401(k) in your current employer's plan, though you won't be able to make further contributions. Other times it can be rolled over into your new employer's plan, or it may be smarter to move it into an individual retirement account.

You should also review your health insurance coverage to see how long it extends after your quit date and what your cost burden for that will be. Insurance through COBRA is often quite pricey since employers aren't required to subsidize its costs like they are for current employees. Check what your current plan would cost through public health insurance marketplaces, as well, which will often be cheaper for short-term coverage between jobs than the post-employment COBRA coverage.

Something else you should check is whether your contract included non-compete or non-disclosure clauses that limit the types of work you can look for. In some cases, these clauses extend months of even years past your departure date, limiting the type of work you can legally look for until that period has elapsed.

<u>3) Plan your quitting timeline.</u>

Some people are able to look for a new job before quitting their current position. For others, this simply isn't feasible with their current schedule, and they will need to determine a timeline for saving up their between-job cushion before quitting. Consider the current demands on your time and how a job search might fit into that, as well as how much you can cut back on current expenses to create a financial cushion during your unemployment. The bottom line is, you want to make sure quitting won't put you in a worse situation than you are in currently. This may mean waiting to quit until 6-12 months into the future, and while that can be frustrating, it is at least often easier to endure the stress and problems in your current job when you know the end is in sight.

Along with your personal finances and schedule, consider the workplace timeline when deciding when to quit. If you get year-end bonuses, for example, you may want to time your departure early in the year so you don't miss out on that extra income. Similarly, find out what happens to unused PTO. Some companies add accrued PTO to your final paycheck, but in other cases you will lose these days, and may not be allowed to use them after you have put in your notice. In this case, your best option may be to use your PTO to get time to start your search so you aren't leaving those benefits on the table.

<u>4) Start your search (discretely).</u>

If you decide it's best for you to have another job in place before quitting, conduct your search outside of work hours. Don't use workplace printers, computers, or supplies for this. While it can feel satisfying to print your resume using the office's paper and ink, that also introduces the risk someone else will see it in the printer tray, and that's an easy way to get your plans spread through the rumor mill. Similarly, if you are searching while still employed, avoid posting your resume publicly on sites like LinkedIn or other job search platforms. It may be better to conduct your search through a recruiter in this case to prevent your current colleagues and managers from finding out you plan to quit until you're ready to tell them.

If you are waiting to look for a new job until after you quit, you can take a few steps in the mean time to give yourself a head start. Update your resume and prepare a list of potential references you can reach out to once you're able. Review your professional network contacts, as well, and determine who you should reach out to about potential opportunities once you're able to publicly discuss your search. Another thing you can do to prepare is clarify exactly what you need from your new job, and what your no-compromise "deal breakers" are. Prepare questions you will ask potential employers during the interview to ensure your new position is an improvement. If you are quitting your current job because of poor or hostile management, for example, asking about the management style, culture, and values during the interview can help you avoid landing in a similar situation.

5) Turn in your resignation letter 2-4 weeks before your last day.

A two-weeks notice is standard professional etiquette to give your company enough time to hire a replacement before you leave. For leadership and specialized positions, a longer notice may be appreciated. Before you write the letter, have a meeting with your direct supervisor to discuss your plans and the timing of your last day. Give them a concise explanation for your resignation, and prepare in advance for what you'll answer if they extend a counter-offer to entice you to stay, or ask for more time to conduct a search for your replacement.

Write your resignation letter shortly after this conversation. It should include your official last day as discussed with your supervisor, as well as other details of your departure like whether you can stay on to train your replacement. Keep the tone of this letter positive and gracious. Thank your employer for the opportunity, and avoid airing any grievances or stating your reasons for quitting—this is information you can discuss in an exit interview or privately with leadership, not something to include in your resignation letter.

6) Reinforce connections with current coworkers and clients.

Once your supervisor and company know you plan to quit, you can share that knowledge with your coworkers. Avoid talking to others in the office about your plans before talking to your boss—you don't want them to hear about it through the grapevine and lose control of your own narrative.

When talking to coworkers and clients, be tactful and modest. You can tell them where you plan to go next, but avoid bragging or bad-mouthing your current workplace. Stay positive in all your interactions, and exchange contact information with the colleagues and clients you want to stay in touch with to maintain the professional connections you've developed during your current employment.

7) Set up your replacement for success.

If you aren't able to stay long enough to train your replacement (or aren't asked to do so by the company), prepare a document of tips, notes, and other advice to leave behind for them, and leave your contact information so they can reach out with any questions they have. Pass any open client contracts or in-progress projects along to coworkers to ensure nothing falls through the cracks during the transition, and make sure your work files are well-organized and well-labeled so they can find information they need after you leave. On your final day, update your company voicemail and email auto-response telling contacts who reach out to you who they should contact instead. The smoother the transition to the new employee, the better that will reflect on you long-term with the company, and the more likely they will be to give you a positive recommendation.

<u>8) Go out on a high note.</u>

First and foremost, continue to show up to work through the last day you've stated. Maintain your usual high standard of work throughout this time and keep all workplace interactions positive and upbeat, even with those individuals who have contributed to your departure. Accept an exit interview if it's offered, and be gracious during this conversation, too. You can share suggestions for improvements during the exit interview, but make sure that criticism is constructive and stick to official workplace business, don't get personal or call out individuals in the office for their behavior. Your main goal in the exit interview shouldn't be to fix all the problems you see in the company; that is no longer your concern. Instead, your focus should be on leaving the team with a good impression of you, so frame all your comments through that lens.

Breaking the Golden Handcuffs

Some jobs are easier to quit than others, and while culture and workplace friendships are a part of this, other companies add a financial aspect by putting their employees in golden handcuffs. This term was first coined by John Steinbeck but has come to describe a job, often one that is stressful and uninspiring but pays well and comes along with perks that are lost if you quit. This could include things like use of a company car, expansive insurance policies, large annual bonuses, or retirement plans that are lost when you leave.

If you think you are caught in golden handcuffs, the first step to breaking free is to assess your spending habits and long-term financial goals. Determine which of your current benefits are actually "above and beyond" and which will likely be replaced, even if in a lesser amount, by whatever job you take next. Stress spending is especially common among those caught in golden handcuffs, so identify those expenses that will no longer be necessary once you have a job with a better work/life balance or lower overall stress levels.

Most jobs that come with golden handcuffs do so for a reason. If your company needs to trap people with perks to make them stay, in many cases it's because their work environment, culture, scheduling demands, or other factors are not conducive to employee mental health. Consider the things you need to do now to safeguard your mental health that won't be necessary once you have a job you enjoy and are doing on your own terms.

The bottom line is, while you should carefully consider your decision to quit your job, finances are just one aspect of the decision, and need to be balanced against your happiness, career progress, and overall wellness. Once you know quitting is the right move, commit to that decision. It may mean making financial sacrifices in the short-term, but those will prove to be an investment in your future when you land a more fulfilling position.

FURTHER READING AND RESOURCES

Online Resources

U.S. Equal Employment Opportunity Commission
https://www.eeoc.gov/
The best resource for U.S.-based workers to find information on employment laws, including those related to discrimination and harassment.

National Conference of State Legislatures
https://www.ncsl.org/research/labor-and-employment.aspx
Information regarding state-level labor laws and employee rights.

Project WHEN
https://projectwhen.org/resources/
A non-profit dedicated to ending workplace harassment, the Project WHEN website has a variety of resources for employees in toxic work environments.

FindLaw
https://www.findlaw.com/employment/legal-help-and-resources.html
An excellent resource for workers to find attorneys that specialize in

employment law. Their site also includes information about state and federal labor laws, the process of hiring an attorney, and other helpful guides related to employee rights.

Society for Human Resource Management (SHRM)
https://www.shrm.org/pages/default.aspx
SHRM is a professional organization for those in HR careers. Their website is an excellent all-purpose resource for managers and employees, and non-members can access most of the guides and information.

Further Reading
Back Off! Your Kick-Ass Guide to Ending Bullying at Work, by Catherine Mattice (Infinity Publishing, 2012).

Rising Above a Toxic Workplace: Taking Care of Yourself in an Unhealthy Environment, by Gary Chapman, Paul White, and Harold Myra (Northfield Publishing, 2014).

Surviving the Toxic Workplace: Protect Yourself Against the Coworkers, Bosses, and Work Environments That Poison Your Day, by Linnda Durre (McGraw Hill, 2010).

Toxic: A guide to rebuilding respect and tolerance in a hostile workplace, by Clive Lewis (Bloomsbury Business, 2021).

RESEARCH SOURCES AND WORKS CITED

"How to Deal With Negative Behavior in the Workplace." *USC Annenberg Master of Communication Management Online*, 23 May 2019. https://communicationmgmt.usc.edu/blog/negative-behavior-work-interventions/.

"Know Your Rights: Experiencing Sexual Harassment at Work." *National Partnership for Women & Families*, March 2019. https://www.nationalpartnership.org/our-work/resources/economic-justice/sexual-harassment/know-your-rights-sexual-harassment-in-the-workplace.pdf.

"News Release: Bureau of Labor Statistics." *U.S. Department of Labor*, 20 January 2022. https://www.bls.gov/news.release/pdf/union2.pdf.

"ZipRecruiter's Gender in the Workplace Survey." *ZipRecruiter Blog*, 5 February 2019. https://www.ziprecruiter.com/blog/ziprecruiter-job-seeker-gender-survey-2018/.

Alnaji, Candace. "6 Ways to Spot a Toxic Direct Report Before They Cause Problems." *FairyGodBoss*, 21 January 2020.

https://fairygodboss.com/articles/6-ways-to-spot-a-toxic-direct-report-before-they-cause-problems.

Barth, Diane. "A Therapist's Advice for Handling An Entitled Co-worker." *Government Executive,* 28 June 2018. https://www.gov-exec.com/management/2018/06/therapists-advice-handling-entitled-coworker/149381/.

Brown, Brené. "Why Setting Boundaries Is Important In the Workplace by Violet Dhu." *Corporate Communication Experts,* 21 January, 2020. https://corporatecommunicationexperts.com.au/setting-boundaries-in-the-workplace/.

Church, Allan H. and Rodney Warrenfeltz. "7 Types of Bad Bosses—And What To Do About Them." *TalentQ,* 11 March 2021. https://www.talent-quarterly.com/7-types-of-bad-bosses-and-what-to-do-about-them/.

Doyle, Alison. "How to Handle an Office Romance." *The Balance Careers,* 12 December 2019. https://www.thebalancecareers.com/how-to-handle-an-office-romance-2059786.

Fast, Nathanael J. "How to Stop the Blame Game." *Harvard Business Review*, 13 May 2010. https://hbr.org/2010/05/how-to-stop-the-blame-game.

Fenton, Matthew K. "Afraid of Losing Your Job? Reporting Harassment in the Workplace." *Wenzel Fenton Cabassa Blog,* 10 May

2021. https://www.wenzelfenton.com/blog/2021/05/10/afraid-of-losing-your-job-reporting-harassment-in-the-workplace/.

Fortin, Drew. "Toxic work environments: 15 factors that create a toxic workplace." *The Predictive Index,* 29 November 2018. https://www.predictiveindex.com/blog/toxic-work-environments-15-signs-of-workplace-toxicity/.

Gallo, Amy. "How to Manage a Toxic Employee." *Harvard Business Review*, 3 October 2016. https://hbr.org/2016/10/how-to-manage-a-toxic-employee.

Gurchiek, Kathy. "Survey: Workplace Friends Important Retention Factor." *Society for Human Resources Management*, 16 December 2014. https://www.shrm.org/resourcesandtools/hr-topics/employee-relations/pages/workplace-friendships.aspx.

Heal, Arran. "What Causes Toxic Workplaces and How to Prevent Them." *Brink: In Practice*, 20 October 2021. https://www.brink-news.com/what-causes-toxic-workplaces-and-how-to-prevent-them/.

Heathfield, Susan M. "How to Deal with a Bully at Work." *The Balance Careers,* 28 February 2021. https://www.thebalancecareers.com/how-to-deal-with-a-bully-at-work-1917901.

Heidrich, Deanne Lee. "Insights into middle managers influence on organisational culture during change: understanding and replicating positive deviance behaviours." *University of Wollongong Research Online,* 2014.

https://ro.uow.edu.au/cgi/viewcontent.cgi?referer=&httpsredir=1&article=5212&context=theses.

Hickok, Hannah. "Why toxic workplace cultures follow you home." *Remote Control,* 4 April 2021. https://www.bbc.com/worklife/article/20210330-why-toxic-workplace-cultures-follow-you-home.

Jackson, T. "What Causes a Toxic Work Environment?" *Asure,* 23 September 2019. https://www.asuresoftware.com/blog/what-causes-toxic-work-environment.

Jeannotte, Julie. "Work-life balance for managers: what does it look like today?" *OfficeVibe,* 14 April 2021. https://officevibe.com/blog/complete-guide-work-life-balance.

Kappel, Mike. "Do You Have a Toxic Employee Wreaking Havoc in Your Business?" *Business.com,* 29 January 2020. https://www.business.com/articles/do-you-have-a-toxic-employee/.

Kivimäki, Mika, et. al. "Long working hours and risk of coronary heart disease and stroke: a systematic review and meta-analysis of published and unpublished data for 603,838 individuals." *The Lancet,* 19 August, 2015. https://www.thelancet.com/journals/lancet/article/PIIS0140-6736(15)60295-1/fulltext.

Larsen, Linda. "How to Excel at Work Without Building Resentment." *Speaking of Women's Health,* 25 July 2018. https://speakingofwomenshealth.com/health-library/how-to-excel-at-work-without-building-resentment.

Lewis, Hayley. "The curse of the middle-manager: How to handle being pulled in every direction and everyone wanting something from you." *LinkedIn*, 7 October 2019, https://www.linkedin.com/pulse/curse-middle-manager-how-handle-being-pulled-every-direction-lewis.

Liu, Cong. "Workplace Ostracism: People's Psychological Attributions and Coping Strategies." *Hofstra Horizons*, 21 May 2020. https://news.hofstra.edu/2020/05/21/workplace-ostracism-peoples-psychological-attributions-coping-strategies/.

Lobell, Kylie Ora. "14 Ways to Quit on Good Terms." *Business News Daily*, 23 September 2021. https://www.businessnewsdaily.com/6116-how-to-quit-your-job-without-burning-bridges.html.

Lucas, Suzanne. "Dear ReWorker: As a Middle Manager, How Can I Improve the Toxic Culture at My Company?" *Cornerstone*, 12 December 2019. https://www.cornerstoneondemand.com/resources/article/dear-reworker-middle-manager-how-can-i-improve-toxic-culture-my-company/

Martinus, Danial. "9 types of toxic coworkers to beware of and how you can deal with them." *Mashable SE Asia*, 2 November 2020. https://sea.mashable.com/culture/13028/9-types-of-toxic-coworkers-and-how-to-deal-with-them.

Marzullo, Dan. "6 Types of Bad Bosses and How to Spot Them in Your Organization." *Zenefits*, 8 January 2021. https://www.zenefits.com/workest/6-types-of-bad-bosses-and-how-to-spot-them-in-your-organization/.

McLeod, Lea. "How to Deal With the 5 Most Negative Types of Coworkers." *The Muse*, 3 January 2014. https://www.themuse.com/advice/how-to-deal-with-the-5-most-negative-types-of-coworkers.

Mizgata, Jennifer. "How middle managers can manage up, down, and still get things done." *Fortune*, 30 January 2020. https://fortune.com/2020/01/30/how-to-manage-up-down-middle-manager-still-be-productive/.

Mollick, Ethan. "People and process, suits and innovators: the role of individual in firm performance." *Strategic Management Journal*, 24 January 2012. http://onlinelibrary.wiley.com/doi/10.1002/smj.1958/full.

Neogy, Rajkumari. "5 strategies to fix a toxic workplace." *Fast Company*, 7 October 2020. https://www.fastcompany.com/90558943/5-strategies-to-fix-a-toxic-workplace.

Nguyen, Steve. "Workplace Friendships: The Benefits and Challenges." *Workplace Psychology*, 7 January 2018. https://workplacepsychology.net/2018/01/07/workplace-friendships-the-benefits-and-challenges/.

O'Connell, Brian. "Shock to the System: Dealing with Toxic

Staffers at Work." *Society of Human Resources Management,* 1 September 2020. https://www.shrm.org/resourcesandtools/hr-topics/people-managers/pages/toxic-workers-cost-money-.aspx.

Olsen, Stephanie. "Caught in the Golden Handcuffs? Here's How to Break Free." *InHerSight,* 13 January 2021. https://www.inher-sight.com/blog/salary/golden-handcuffs.

Porath, Christine. "How to Avoid Hiring a Toxic Employee." *Harvard Business Review,* 3 February 2016. https://hbr.org/2016/02/how-to-avoid-hiring-a-toxic-employee.

Porath, Christine and Christine Pearson. "The Price of Incivility." *Harvard Business Review Magazine,* January-February 2013.

Priesemuth, Manuela. "Time's up for Toxic Workplaces." *Harvard Business Review,* 19 June 2020. https://hbr.org/2020/06/times-up-for-toxic-workplaces.

Prins, Seth J. et. al. "Anxious? Depressed? You might be suffering from capitalism: contradictory class locations and the prevalence of depression and anxiety in the USA." *Sociology of Health & Illness,* 3 August 2015. http://onlinelibrary.wiley.com/doi/10.1111/1467-9566.12315/full.

Reed, Rachel. "Pros & Cons of Work Spouse Relationships." *Rewardian Blog,* 4 January 2018. https://blog.rewardian.com/pros-cons-of-work-spouse-relationships.

Rigglo, Ronald E. "How to Fix a Toxic Work Culture." *Psychology Today*, 20 June 2021. https://www.psychologytoday.com/us/blog/cutting-edge-leadership/202106/how-fix-toxic-work-culture.

Rosenberg McKay, Dawn. "Is It Time to Quit Your Job?" *The Balance Careers*, 25 June 2019. https://www.thebalancecareers.com/is-it-time-to-quit-your-job-526136.

Rothbard, Nancy. "Is Your Workplace Tough—or Is It Toxic?" *Knowledge at Wharton*, 12 August 2015. https://knowledge.wharton.upenn.edu/article/is-your-workplace-tough-or-is-it-toxic/.

Rothbard, Nancy. "Managing the Dark Side of Workplace Friendships." *Knowledge at Wharton*, 24 April 2018. https://knowledge.wharton.upenn.edu/article/managing-the-dark-side-of-workplace-friendships/.

Schooley, Skye. "Workplace Harassment: How to Recognize and Report It." *Business News Daily*, 21 December 2021. https://www.businessnewsdaily.com/9426-workplace-harassment.html.

Schwantes, Marcel. "5 Signs to Immediately Recognize a Toxic Boss in Action." *Inc.*, 28 February 2021. https://www.inc.com/marcel/schwantes/toxic-boss-signs.html.

Schwantes, Marcel. "These 6 Red Flags Indicate a Toxic Hybrid Workplace." *Inc.*, 25 June 2021. https://www.inc.com/marcel-schwantes/these-6-red-flags-indicate-a-toxic-hybrid-workplace.html.

Sonini, Lucas. "5 Ways to Know If You Are Hiring a Toxic Employee." *Crosschq*, 26 April 2021.
https://www.crosschq.com/blog/2021/04/27/5-ways-to-know-if-you-are-hiring-a-toxic-employee/.

Stevens, Paris. "Happiness in the Workplace Survey." *Wildgoose*, 9 June 2021. https://wearewildgoose.com/uk/news/friends-happiness-in-the-workplace-survey/.

Stillman, Jessica. "5 Signs You Need to Work on Setting Boundaries, According to a Psychotherapist." *Inc*, 17 November 2020. https://www.inc.com/jessica-stillman/boundary-setting-annie-wright-steve-jobs.html.

Torres, Monica. "How smart people react when others take credit for their work." *The Ladders*, 13 June 2017. https://www.theladders.com/career-advice/others-take-credit-for-work.

Trevino, Richard. "The 5 'Cs' Approach to Conflict Resolution in the Workplace." *Entrepreneur*, 10 June 2020. https://www.entrepreneur.com/article/350374.

Tripathi, Sumedha. "13 Signs That Tell You Your Boss Is Toxic." *India Times*, 22 September 2021.
https://www.indiatimes.com/trending/social-relevance/signs-that-your-boss-is-toxic-547960.html.

Vasel, Kathryn. "How to financially prepare to quit your job." *CNN Business*, 24 November 2021. https://www.cnn.com/2021/11/24/success/financial-impact-quit-job-feseries/index.html.

Weiss, Mallory. "How to Fix a Toxic Workplace." *Ethena Blog*, 21 September 2021. https://www.goethena.com/post/how-to-fix-a-toxic-workplace.

Wood, Johnny. "Why it's good to turn your colleagues into friends." *World Economic Forum*, 22 November, 2019. https://www.weforum.org/agenda/2019/11/friends-relationships-work-productivity-career/.

Wood, Kendall. "How to Spot a Bad Egg in the Office." *Bustle*, 25 October 2016. https://www.bustle.com/articles/188879-11-habits-toxic-coworkers-have-in-common-to-watch-out-for-in-the-office.

Zadow, Amy Jane, et. al. "Predicting new major depression symptoms from long working hours, psychosocial safety climate and work engagement: a population-based cohort study." *BMJ Journals*, 23 June 2021. https://bmjopen.bmj.com/content/11/6/e044133.

Ziv, Staf. "Don't Let Workplace Bullies Win—Here's How to Spot Them and Stop Them." *The Muse*, 28 March 2019. https://www.themuse.com/advice/how-to-deal-with-workplace-bullies.